Democracy:
A World History

The
New
Oxford
World
History

Democracy:
A World History

Temma Kaplan

OXFORD

UNIVERSITY PRESS

OXFORD
UNIVERSITY PRESS

Oxford University Press is a department of the University of
Oxford. It furthers the University's objective of excellence in research,
scholarship, and education by publishing worldwide.

Oxford   New York
Auckland   Cape Town   Dar es Salaam   Hong Kong   Karachi
Kuala Lumpur   Madrid   Melbourne   Mexico City   Nairobi
New Delhi   Shanghai   Taipei   Toronto

With offices in
Argentina   Austria   Brazil   Chile   Czech Republic   France   Greece
Guatemala   Hungary   Italy   Japan   Poland   Portugal   Singapore
South Korea   Switzerland   Thailand   Turkey   Ukraine   Vietnam

Oxford is a registered trademark of Oxford University Press
in the UK and certain other countries.

Published in the United States of America by
Oxford University Press
198 Madison Avenue, New York, NY 10016

© Oxford University Press 2015

Library of Congress Cataloging-in-Publication Data
Kaplan, Temma, 1942–
Democracy : a world history / Temma Kaplan.
pages cm
Includes bibliographical references and index
ISBN 978-0-19-517676-6 (hardback);   978-0-19-533808-9 (paperback)
1. Democracy—History.   2. World politics.   I. Title.
JC421.K365 2015
321.8—dc23
2014028716

*Frontispiece: Women voting in Japan. Library of Congress,
LC-DIG-ggbain-34126*

Contents

Editors' Preface

This book is part of the New Oxford World History, an innovative series that offers readers an informed, lively, and up-to-date history of the world and its people that represents a signifi cant change from the "old" world history. Only a few years ago, world history generally amounted to a history of the West—Europe and the United States—with small amounts of information from the rest of the world. Some versions of the "old" world history drew attention to every part of the world *except* Europe and the United States. Readers of that kind of world history could get the impression that somehow the rest of the world was made up of exotic people who had strange customs and spoke difficult languages. Still another kind of "old" world history presented the story of areas or peoples of the world by focusing primarily on the achievements of great civilizations. One learned of great buildings, influential world religions, and mighty rulers but little of ordinary people or more general economic and social patterns. Interactions among the world's peoples were often told from only one perspective.

This series tells world history differently. First, it is comprehensive, covering all countries and regions of the world and investigating the total human experience—even those of so-called peoples without histories living far from the great civilizations. "New" world historians thus share in common an interest in all of human history, even going back millions of years before there were written human records. A few "new" world histories even extend their focus to the entire universe, a "big history" perspective that dramatically shifts the beginning of the story back to the big bang. Some see the "new" global framework of world history today as viewing the world from the vantage point of the Moon, as one scholar put it. We agree. But we also want to take a closeup view, analyzing and reconstructing the significant experiences of all of humanity.

This is not to say that everything that has happened everywhere and in all time periods can be recovered or is worth knowing, but that there is much to be gained by considering both the separate and interrelated stories of different societies and cultures. Making these connections is still another crucial ingredient of the "new" world history. It emphasizes connectedness and interactions of all kinds—cultural, economic, political, religious, and social—involving peoples, places, and processes. It makes comparisons and finds similarities. Emphasizing both the comparisons and interactions is critical to developing a global framework that can deepen and broaden historical understanding, whether the focus is on a specific country or region or on the whole world.

The rise of the new world history as a discipline comes at an opportune time. The interest in world history in schools and among the general public is vast. We travel to one another's nations, converse and work with people around the world, and are changed by global events. War and peace affect populations worldwide as do economic conditions and the state of our environment, communications, and health and medicine. The New Oxford World History presents local histories in a global context and gives an overview of world events seen through the eyes of ordinary people. This combination of the local and the global further defines the new world history. Understanding the workings of global and local conditions in the past gives us tools for examining our own world and for envisioning the interconnected future that is in the making.

Bonnie G. Smith
Anand Yang

Introduction

In 1947, Winston Churchill, the Prime Minister of Great Britain during the Second World War, told a session of Parliament that "democracy is the worst form of government except [for] all the others that have been tried from time to time."[1] This book explores the many meanings of democracy as it has developed in both small groups and large populations over most of human history.

Simply stated, democracy is a process through which people confer with each other to secure food, shelter, land, water, and peace for their mutual benefit. As groups of people grow larger, they usually form specialized committees to meet particular challenges. Although political relationships always depend on group survival, their study seldom considers the provision of physical resources such as land and water as this book does.

As a set of practices associated with the rule of law and widespread participation in administering that law, democracies have developed for thousands of years all over the world. But as diverse as democracies have been, the people who generate laws and those who attempt to create, maintain, or change the laws and practices that permit people to live together in peace have been relatively exclusive and nearly impossible to sustain over long periods. In order to protect those recognized as citizens, most known democracies have considered at least some people as outsiders and have excluded them from the benefits of democracy and citizenship. The existence of democracy among one group does not necessarily lead to the empowerment of all residents or their inclusion in common deliberations. And the decisions made directly or by representatives may rule unfairly against any group that lacks its own representation. It is important to remember that, in practice, democracies can carry out atrocities against as well as grant benefits to large numbers of people.

If democracies are no better than tyrannies or dictatorships, then why focus on democracy at all and why associate democracy with freedom, as so many patriots have done? The attraction of democracy is that it raises possibilities for creating what the nineteenth-century British philosopher Jeremy Bentham called "the greatest happiness for the greatest number." By the sheer quantity of ideas people reasoning together can promote, democracies increase the chances of achieving peace, justice, and social benefits for all. But, democracy has never come easily and its only chance for gaining what it, more than any other set of practices, might achieve, is by making it ever more inclusive. Since democracy never rests and must continuously be re-created and protected, it is always unstable and threatened with extinction.

With that long struggle in mind, ninety-three-year-old Frances Baard, who had already spent most of her life fighting to be a citizen in the country where she was born, voted for the first time in South Africa in 1994. She had joined with others in demonstrating against unjust laws, had fought to win the rights she and other workers required, had struggled to retain her freedom when charged with resisting unjust laws, and had campaigned against carrying passes that acted as internal passports forbidding her to live and work in certain places. Although casting her vote was one of the high points of her life, voting merely marked the culmination of a life devoted to winning what she considered to be democracy.

For those who think that democracy simply entails citizens electing governments that rule through representative institutions according to specific legal codes or constitutions, Baard represents the activists who have shaped democracy for thousands of years. During that time, democracy has referred to a variety of ideals, legal systems, associations, political practices, institutions, and social movements in which various people have united to gain the individual and collective freedom that they need to survive and live together in equality and peace. This second category of democracy, known as direct or participatory democracy, includes local movements and decision-making processes of ordinary people, whether or not they are considered full citizens; they create organizations to uphold laws and rules they consider vital; they form social movements in order to win the democratic rights they desire; and they construct systems to control natural resources and the economy for their mutual benefit. At one time or another, each form of democracy has had to partake in choosing rulers, formulating policy, creating legal codes and judicial processes, and organizing public assemblies and organizations.

Like other governmental forms, democracies often fail in their professed goals. At various times, democracies have excluded or discriminated against people of particular castes, classes, religions, nationalities, ethnicities, sexual groups, and races, as the original Constitution of the United States did when it counted black slaves as three-fifths of a person. But the existence of democracy in even the smallest group usually persuades women, people of color, suppressed minorities or majorities, and other excluded groups to demand their rights to participate as equal citizens of every community. And, as we will see in this book, movements for democratic systems and struggles for the expansion of democratic rights have long motivated people and their communities around the world, leading many to consciously risk their lives in order to realize this powerful ideal.

Both representative and participatory democracy have generated written codes designed to prevent the stealing of land or water; or ending torture, enslavement, and false imprisonment; or advancing freedom of religion or freedom from state religions. Both systems of democracy have enhanced free expression, human rights, and, perhaps, most importantly, freedom of speech and publication, necessary for the maintenance of public life. Periodically, individuals and communities of almost all races, sexes, and ethnicities have attempted to govern themselves, secure precious resources, move freely, and shape their own lives.

Accompanying democracy's achievements, most democracies have historically had two fatal flaws: one is the lack of effective routine communication between elected officials and ordinary people needed to share ideas and work out conflicts. The other is that democracies, like authoritarian governments, have tendencies that reach toward expansionism. Even in efforts to grant citizenship and extend democratic rights to previously excluded groups of former slaves, immigrants, and people of different ethnic origins, for example, most democracies have imposed themselves on others, colonizing them and dislodging or suppressing original inhabitants. Often, conflicts even within established democracies have also led to oppressive conditions for some of the population. Recent access to the internet and social media provides a new and important way to link ordinary people to those who wield political power, but it also presents authorities with powerful tools to manipulate public opinion. Although democracy seems easy to take for granted, humans have not found a guaranteed way to create and permanently preserve democracy. Yet, despite democracy's many failures, it remains a stirring dream, a fantasy, an ideal that has taken various institutional forms over time and generated hopes for creating equitable social, economic, and political arrangements now and in the future.

Though few democratic systems have sustained themselves effectively for very long, their periodic emergence nearly everywhere on earth over thousands of years indicates the resilience despite the fragility of the democratic ideal. Rather than viewing democracy as simply an unrealizable goal, many people regard democracy as an infinitely changeable set of processes, a creative form of life that distinguishes humans from all other living beings. For these reasons as well as the periodic recognition that there has to be some political alternative to the political systems under which most people live, various claims for democracy have emerged throughout history.

CHAPTER 1

Parting the Waters and Organizing the People

Ancient democracy depended on the ability of people to supplement hunting and gathering with farming, which required regular access to water. In fact, the need to share water required settlers of any kind to take responsibility for their own actions and collaborate with their neighbors to direct the flow of water and distribute it to canals, water basins, and sluices. In the Fertile Crescent of Mesopotamia in contemporary Iraq, a network of canals brought the waters of the Tigris-Euphrates together to irrigate the surrounding fields.

Attempts to control the distribution of water appear for the first time in a code of law written for King Hammurabi of Babylonia, Mesopotamia, between 1792 and 1750 before the Common Era (BCE), 450 years before the Ten Commandments appeared. The threat of floods in the Fertile Crescent required constant vigilance not only of overseers, but of ordinary farmers who rented or sharecropped their land. Their own survival depended on working with neighbors to maintain the dikes and keep sluices in good order, and this code of law enforced a trajectory of local people working for their mutual benefit. Those individuals and groups charged with overseeing bridges, ports, and canals might incur sanctions if they attempted to advance their own interests over those of their neighbors. And the code encouraged farmers to improve the use of waterways and control how water was distributed. For example, the code mandated that "if any one open his ditches to water his crop, but is careless, and the water flood[s] the field of his neighbor, then he shall pay his neighbor corn [wheat] for his loss. . . ." Furthermore, "if he be not able to replace the corn, then he and his possessions shall be divided among the farmers whose corn he has flooded."[1] Punishments were even harsher for those whose dams were not kept up: "if any one be too lazy to keep his dam in proper condition, and does not so keep it; if then the dam break and all the fields be flooded, then shall he in whose dam the break occurred be sold for money, and the money shall replace the corn which he has caused to be ruined."[2]

Hammurabi's Code could inflict cruel sentences, but, although it and subsequent laws were imposed without any popular participation in decision-making, the code that appeared on stone tablets in a public place proclaimed a certain level of cooperation for which people were responsible.

Just as Mesopotamia depended on regulating the Tigris and Euphrates, the Moche state along the northwest coast of contemporary Perú seems to have galvanized certain people to band together to regulate the scarce water supplies. The culture that by the 15th century of the Common Era (CE) had developed a centralized political authority first formed between 1800 and 1500 BCE on the dry land of the narrow desert valleys between the high mountains. According to archeological evidence, in times of peace or extended drought, unidentified farmers formed local groups to design and construct irrigation canals as well

This inscribed stele or post from about 1750 BCE shows Shamash, the Mesopotamian god of justice and of the sun, with King Hammurabi. Hammurabi's Code, which the god conferred on the king, was intended, according to its prologue, "to bring about the rule of righteousness" and "to destroy the wicked and the evil doers so that the strong should not harm the weak" so that Hammurabi would "enlighten the land to further the well-being of mankind." Louvre, Paris, © RMN-Grand Palais / Art Resource, NY

as to organize religious rituals.[3] These local associations to coordinate efforts and resolve differences seem to have become stronger between 200 and 800 CE, during the middle and high Moche period. Sometimes the need to regulate water brought mutually antagonistic groups into coalitions with one another so that unified states alternated with small, self-governing units in the Jequetepeque Valley. During the so-called Middle Moche period, members of the local communities united and possibly formed self-governing bodies to plan and construct four new canals in order to expand the farmland available to them all.

A similar and more easily documented pattern developed among the Maya people of contemporary Yucatan, Mexico, southwestern Guatemala, and northwestern Honduras. According to anthropologists, a so-called "Cargo System" of sharing responsibility emerged at various times between 350 BCE and 700 CE in much of what we now know as Southern Mexico and Central America. Although this whole area was generally dominated by kings, other men who by birth or by talent were designated to fulfill certain tasks for a period up to a year often rose to power as local lords, and sometimes even contended with kings. In times of crisis due to drought or threats from neighboring settlements, the kings sometimes had to summon the local dignateries to form a council, as the lord of Copán in Honduras is thought to have done in the mid-eighth century CE after his predecessor was murdered.[4] The council seems to have held their meetings in the so-called Popol Nah or Council House commissioned in Copán in 776 CE.

Even in ancient Egypt where the Pharaohs ruled between 1550 and 1070 BCE, there seems to have been local participation in control of the Nile.[5] What remained of the water after the large estates received their share flowed to the sluices, water basins, and the fields of local farms. Little is known about the ways the smaller cultivators created the water basins to store the water, constructed the canals, or built the dikes that protected the fields from the overflow of the river, but the work seems to have been widely decentralized, requiring a degree of cooperation that demanded consultation among those controlling the water.[6] Participation in the distribution of water may have shaped other social and religious relationships as well. As in Mesopotamia, those who were careful not to take more than their share by building dams or otherwise diverting water for personal gain rather than promoting the collective good could expect rewards in the afterlife.[7] If the prehistory of democracy undoubtedly took place around life-and-death issues such as the management of water, full-blown democratic institutions and practices flourished in ancient Greece, particularly in Athens.

From the seventh through the fourth century BCE, Athens established precedent after precedent for both representative and participatory democracy. As in ancient Mesopotamia, the stories of the great lawgivers help form what we know about democracy. Solon and Pericles allegedly shaped democratic lawmaking by promoting activities that were being undertaken collectively in the *agora* or public market of ideas and institutionalized in the Assembly, the most democratic of all public institutions. Without doubt, from the perspectives of both representative and direct democracy, something exceptional occurred in Athens. In fact, the wonder of Athenian democracy was the creation of multiple venues in which ordinary citizens—albeit limited only to men and excluding women, slaves, and outsiders—could act for the common good.

Without romanticizing Athenian democracy or underestimating its failures, the Athenian city-state's ability to provide far-reaching opportunities for ordinary citizens to initiate laws, shape policy, and adjudicate disputes to establish new political opportunities made it distinctive for many reasons. By the sixth century BCE, most of what is contemporary Greece had been organized into city-states where kings and aristocrats, some of whom bore responsibility for carrying out religious rituals, ruled.

Greece consisted of discrete enclaves on which agriculture was difficult and residents turned to the sea for their livelihood. Despite being surrounded by water, Athens in particular piped water into its towns and fields to supplement the water it secured from nearby wells and springs. Part of the sense of community Greeks developed from the eighth century BCE on was due to the democratic distribution of water. Apart from the growing wealth of the Athenian empire in the fifth century BCE, the silver mines worked by slaves contributed to the well-being of those who were citizens. Citizens and resident foreigners, known as *metis*, lived in *demes* or neighborhoods in the *polis* or city-state in which farmers, craftsmen, shopkeepers, and small merchants shared moderate forms of civic life, and the entire population was concerned with the availability and provision of water.

From the seventh through the fifth century BCE, Athenian dependence on naval power may have promoted democracy. Athens could not have survived without grain from Ukraine, one reason that Athens feared Persian movements toward the Dardanelles, the Bosporus, and the Black Sea, and maybe the main reason Athens extended so many rights of participatory democracy to lower-class male citizens who served in its navy. Though nobles ruled, they were constrained by legal codes and various juries, assemblies, and councils made up of ordinary male citizens committed to the rule of law. On a rotating basis they chose judges and formed committees to study the meaning of laws and apply them in individual cases.[8]

The Greeks increasingly insisted on writing down laws and diffusing power in order to reduce the possibility of tyrants seizing power. With the constant threat of civil war, noble families who ruled Athens called on aristocrats such as the poet Solon, who lived roughly between 640 and 560 BCE, to consolidate disparate laws. Although such a figure existed, little is known about what he actually wrote or accomplished, but he is credited with having changed marriage laws. Portrayed in legends as a wise leader, he was known for mediating between the rich and the poor. So, for example, when asked his opinion about well-run cities, he described one as "that city where those who have not been injured take up the cause of one who has, and prosecute the case as earnestly as if the wrong had been done to themselves."[9] His alleged efforts to reduce the cost of dowries, inhibit forced marriages of heiresses to male relatives, permit citizens to have others aid them in legal matters, and appeal judgments to groups representing the larger community, would have granted wider representation to most Athenians. Solon supposedly wanted the poor as well as the rich to participate in government and allowed the lowest class, the *thetes*, to serve on the jury of the assembly. Whether or not the laws Solon decreed were intentionally ambiguous, many believe that the room they left for interpretation granted the lowest class great power. Another change that occurred during Solon's rule was the creation of the Council of 400, a group that generated the proposals that were discussed and voted on by the people of all ranks gathered in the Assembly.[10]

The Assembly, which first began meeting in the sixth century BCE, on the Pnyx hill near the Acropolis, was the wonder of Greek democracy. Despite other achievements, few democratic institutions anywhere else have ever equaled its level of participatory democracy. The Assembly consisted of six thousand male citizens, including masons, carpenters, and merchants, and met at least forty times a year for one-day sessions. Although it excluded women, slaves, and foreign immigrants, at the height of its power in the fifth century BCE, the Assembly was open to 35,000–40,000 men over eighteen years of age. Even people from the countryside were eligible to participate, though farmers seldom appeared even when, as in the fourth century BCE, all members of the Assembly are thought to have been paid for participating. The stipend was equal to only half a mason's daily wage, but paying anything for services assured that even poor men might theoretically be able to join the Assembly and consider the issues of the day. Once the per diem was introduced, the Assembly attracted the old, indigent, and lower-paid people, skewing its membership overwhelmingly toward people of the lower classes.[11]

Even so, the principal leaders of democracy, such as Pericles of Athens, came from the elite, who studied speaking techniques known as rhetoric. Under Pericles's leadership, the Assembly dominated the older aristocratic branch of government, the Council of 500 (previously the Council of 400), which controlled the military and generated legislation. As Pericles said, "Our constitution is called a democracy because power is in the hands not of a minority but of the whole people. When it is a question of settling private disputes, everyone is equal before the law; when it is a question of putting one person before another in positions of public responsibility, what counts is not membership of a particular class, but the actual ability which the man possesses."[12] The courts and city officials (chosen by lottery) brought adversaries together to resolve their differences. If mediation failed, a jury—which was also selected by lottery and, from the fifth century BCE on, paid for their services—adjudicated the cases. By that time, in mixing older institutions that had survived over generations with newer, autonomous local organizations that allowed participants to meet new challenges, Greece united popular and representative democratic forms.

But then, and as would occur again later, democracy faced disintegration due to war. Persistent wars that pitted Athenians against Persians and then against the united forces of the Greek Peloponnese led by Sparta promoted increased centralization of power. This led to the decreasing influence of popular democracy in the Assembly. The exigencies of war precluded the slow and deliberative discussions that took place among the tens of thousands of men in the Assembly. Moreover, the need for secrecy meant that public discussion of strategy often curtailed popular democracy in the Assembly, eventually leading to Athenian submission to Spartan rule, and then, in 338 BCE, to Philip II of Macedonia and his son, Alexander the Great. Imperialism and the decreasing ability of citizens to participate in making major political decisions undermined Athenian democracy despite the cultural advances that Athens made under Socrates, Plato, and Aristotle in the fifth century BCE. While Plato and presumably Socrates, whose philosophical ideas Plato conveyed, believed that monarchy, not democracy, was the superior form of rule, Aristotle, who surveyed various systems, thought that democracy was the ultimate model of good government. But not if there was constant warfare as was the case in Greece from the fifth century onward. And the Greeks' failure was the world's loss.

Many speculate about the extent to which democratic governments or major democratic practices existed during the thousand years that followed Greece's decline. Others doubt whether the Roman Republic was ever democratic at all. Even though Rome liked to view itself as the heir to ancient Greece, and could boast about the rights of citizens to vote in elections, deliberate in noncapital court cases, and initiate new laws—practices the Romans developed between 139 and 130 BCE— this might not have been enough for some to consider their system democratic. The early republic that lasted roughly from 509 to 287 BCE gave birth to a series of institutions that might have resulted in periods of moderate self-government, among patricians, whose ancestors may have fulfilled religious duties or occupied political positions. Whatever their origins, wealthy patricians generally filled the ranks of the Senate. While a small minority of lower-class men (known as plebeians) who had achieved a certain level of wealth were able to occupy high posts in the military, most plebeians were poor farmers and city dwellers.

The first Roman legal code, known as the Twelve Tables, seems to have been generated between 451 and 450 BCE and was hung on bronze plaques in the Roman Forum to alert patricians and plebeians about their rights. Its single most important difference from Hammurabi's Code and Solon's reforms was that the Twelve Tables permitted men to be sold into slavery for going deeply in debt. Even with the Twelve Tables, it was not until 287 BCE, when the Tribal Assembly was established, that those outside of the elite seem to have gained any rights to write laws or carry on legal proceedings.

The one major democratic advance in Rome was in the creation of public advocates, called Tribunes, who received no salaries, but looked out for the interest of the plebeians. Although the Tribunes themselves were generally the children of the wealthy men who dominated the Roman Senate, the Tribunes had veto power over proposals the Senate offered.

Two of the few efforts at ruling democratically came during the period when Tiberius Gracchus served as Tribune in 133 BCE, and, nine years after his death, when his younger brother, Gaius Gracchus, assumed that post. Rome had gradually extended its territory, first, to the North African city-state of Carthage, against which it had fought three successive wars, and later to Greece, Asia Minor, and the Middle East. Rome's wars against supposed enemies brought in new lands that

This bronze relief of Tiberius and Gaius Gracchi shows two of the most important republican reformers in second century BCE Rome. The Gracchi brothers tried to reduce the power of slave-holding senators, distribute newly conquered land to the landless, and extend Roman citizenship to people in surrounding territories. The assassinations of the two brothers marked the demise of the Roman Republic and the beginning of imperial rule. Photo courtesy Musée d'Orsay, Paris, RMN-Grand Palais / Art Resource, NY

were generally sold to the richest citizens, but some of the territory was turned into common lands that the poorest farmers could rent. The rich quickly began to encroach on these properties, as well, until the government decreed that no one person could hold more than a thousand acres. Since owning land as well as weapons qualified men to serve in the military, the distribution of some conquered territory to the poorer farmers also expanded the number of men eligible for military service in the Roman legions.

By the time Tiberius Gracchus came to power as Tribune in 133 BCE, the great landowners had increased their holdings beyond the thousand acres permitted by law. Gracchus, himself a veteran of the wars in Carthage, argued that "the savage beasts in Italy, have their particular dens, they have their places of repose and refuge; but the men who bear arms, and expose their lives for the safety of their country, enjoy in the meantime nothing more in it but the air and light and, having no houses or settlements of their own, are constrained to wander from place to place with their wives and children."[13] Tiberius Gracchus's attempt to enforce the rule limiting holdings to a thousand acres cost him his life. The King of Pergamum, a rich settlement on the Turkish coast, lacking an heir, willed his entire kingdom to the Roman Republic in hope that his donation would prevent a bloody civil war from occurring after his death. Tiberius Gracchus thought that some of this land should be given to poor farmers to cultivate in common, a view so radically democratic that the Senate, with the support of one of the Tribunes, sent three thousand armed men to Capitol Hill to murder Tiberius and his followers.[14]

A similar fate befell his younger brother, Gaius Gracchus, when he attempted to allow poor Romans to attain land in the recently conquered territories and permit Roman commoners to serve on juries.[15] Fully embracing Roman imperialism, Gaius Gracchus nevertheless wanted to extend its benefits to the newly expanding commercial groups, veterans, and the poor. He also suggested strengthening the empire by granting full citizenship, including rights of marriage, to so-called Latins and Italians from northern Italy, which lay outside the proper boundaries of Rome. This proposal faced opposition from the Senate and the popular classes who considered themselves the only true Romans since incorporating alleged outsiders would not only have increased the size of the electorate, but would also have diminished the power of the Senate. When Gaius took the unusual step of running for a second term in 122 BCE, his enemies killed him. While even the pretense of a democratic government disappeared with the accession of Octavian, known as Augustus, paradoxically, the reforms of the Gracchus brothers, based as they were on extending democratic rights through imperial expansion, helped to provide imperialism with a democratic tinge.

The decline of the Roman Empire entailed the increased importance of customary law that both enhanced and diminished the possibilities for democracy. Rome's decline also resulted from widespread population movements including those of the Germanic peoples into lands previously occupied by Rome. Rome's continuous warfare, increasingly dependent on armies made up of people for whom imperial expansion was a livelihood, contributed to its decline. Former provinces and frontier societies broke off and formed independent communities, some of which attempted to govern themselves relatively democratically. In northern Europe, provinces that had formerly paid allegiance to Rome now formed their own governing units. Some in the north were cut off from long-distance trade as urban life declined. The regions bordering on the Mediterranean continued to trade with one another, but commerce became more and more unstable as pirates hijacked goods sent from one place to another. For about eight centuries, northern Europe turned inward, as people fled the cities and retreated to the countryside to produce food.

For several centuries following Rome's decline, religious communities dominated civic life. Almost all the great religious movements—Judaism, Christianity, Islam, Buddhism, Confucianism, and Zoroastrianism—generated communitarian impulses, especially in their initial stages. Although the Scripture shared by Jews, Christians, and Muslims as "people of the book," was widely open to interpretation, the notion of a covenant with God provided a contractual foundation for all three religions. In accounting for time in Egypt (roughly 1300 BCE), the ancient Hebrews viewed themselves as people governed according to laws that Moses and other prophets secured for them. In the Ten Commandments, followers of all three religions learned, as secular groups in Babylonia had learned from Hammurabi's Code, how they should try to comport themselves. All three people of the book developed precepts for conducting good lives, but all of them had tendencies to accept the authority of patriarchal elders to rule over the community.

The early followers of Jesus of Nazareth, as radical reformers, proponents of the equality of all souls, and opponents of the political and religious rule of the Romans, seemed to some later followers to be speaking the language of democracy. For them, this entailed the equal participation of the poor, the weak, the scorned, and the denigrated who gathered together in a community that served God. In a series of aphorisms, Jesus the Carpenter and his followers represented the workers, the poor, thieves, prostitutes, and all the wretched of the earth. This interpretation, which has periodically re-emerged, focuses on forming communities of equals joined together to worship God and administer good works. As Christianity spread from Palestine to the rest of the Roman Empire, there is no doubt that the early Christians united in small, largely self-governing communities where both men and women fully participated. As late as the fourth century BCE, North African born St. Augustine continued to judge Christians by their ability to integrate large numbers into a political community. In fact, Augustine thought that Christianity represented a superior "republic" to Rome since it was capable of achieving "true justice" by linking participatory democracy with the revelation of God's word.[16]

Muhammad, a merchant born in Mecca in 570 CE in what is now Saudi Arabia, was drawn to the teaching of Jewish and Christian people, especially their emphasis on monotheism and law uniting disparate groups. Three great monotheistic religions emerged from the Hebrew Bible, each building on earlier ideals about the need to create a community of worshippers, but each had similar tendencies toward hierarchical priesthoods and centralizing policies. Muhammad, like Jesus, was surrounded by an inner circle that constituted a political community that initially transcended kinship networks or a sense of superiority over other monotheistic religions. Muhammad's immediate successors, including Abu Bakr, the first Caliph, who died in 634 CE, and his successor, Umar, ruled through somewhat democratic councils. The center of Islamic political rule was the *umma*, or community, that wielded religious and political authority over people previously governed by tribal relationships. Controversies periodically ensued over the power of the *imam*, the spiritual leader of the community, and whether or how he spoke for the umma. Different dynasties followed one another ruling a territory that by 750 CE extended from the Indus River in India to the Guadalquivir, Tajo, and Ebro Rivers in Spain.

In the eighth century in Oman, Muslims attempted to limit the power of rulers to prevent them from becoming tyrants at the same time that the Frankish Kingdoms of the West were developing a highly centralized monarchy under Charlemagne and his successors. Like the ancient Greeks, many Muslims from the eighth to the eleventh centuries feared the emergence of tyrants and preferred easily replaced imams to those whose family connections or even personal wisdom set them apart and made them harder to remove. The Mu'tazilites of Basra and Baghdad, in what is today Iraq, were even willing to contemplate a world without any imams, especially if those imams periodically commanded enough power to become virtual kings. Once Muhammad and his son-in-law Ali were dead, assemblies of peers might have done a better job than any single imam, or might have merely served the community as Muhammad's aides were thought to have done. Al-Aṣamm, a ninth century Mu'tazilite writer, thought that councils rather than single imams should have simply met periodically to solve common problems. And Al-Aṣamm even went as far as to suggest that each province could have its own imam, who might unite with others in federations to govern the larger community.[17]

Some Muslims apparently shared ancient Greeks' fears that even esteemed leaders might easily turn into tyrants, and such anxieties undoubtedly played a role in certain Muslim translations of Greek political thought, including the works of Aristotle on democracy. The revival of Aristotle's *Politics* in thirteenth-century Europe and North Africa seems to have played a role in promoting the ideal of political community as central to human life.[18] From the thirteenth to the fourteenth centuries, Jewish and Christian scholars translated these works from Arabic into Hebrew and Latin, re-establishing them as central tenets of Western thought. In Al Andalus, the name the Muslims gave to Southern Spain, they debated the merits of democracy according to the Greeks, but they also helped reintroduce Roman law that supported the contrary tendency of enhancing opportunities for secular and religious leaders to expand their powers.

Unfortunately, democratic gains for some can often come at the expense of diminished freedom for others, particularly when one group takes over the other's territory. In the Middle Ages, Christians from northern Spain expanded into the territories held by Muslims in the south and Christians from what is today Germany conquered the Wends in the areas east of the Elbe River. For example, as Christian forces moved south from their small kingdoms in northern Spain to carry out what subsequent historians mislabeled a "Reconquest" of lands that had been settled by ancient Iberians, Phoenicians, Romans, Jews, Visigoths, and later people from contemporary Syria, Iran, Iraq, and North Africa, the northern Christian Kings offered self-governing rights in charters, or *fueros*, to those who agreed to repopulate the cities and towns and the surrounding land. As such, the Spanish Christians succeeded in conquering people whom they regarded as heathens and replacing them with loyal citizens of Christian city-states.

On Europe's eastern frontier, the Teutonic and Livonian Knights, who were members of militarized religious orders, attempted from the twelfth century on to spread Christianity from medieval German territories that had been part of the eastern holdings of Charlemagne and his successors into Prussia and what became the Baltic states east of the Elbe River. Like their Spanish brethren, these German military orders were willing to offer settlers contractual rights and privileges in exchange for leaving friends, families, and familiar territory to move east. Like later settlers in the United States, Australia, Argentina, and South Africa, those who bettered themselves by abandoning their home territories in the Middle Ages sought rights and privileges for themselves, but did not have any intention of extending those rights to the indigenous groups they displaced.

Kings also gained and lost powers to govern as a result of charters. As early as the Norman Conquest of 1066 CE, the kings of England conferred with their barons, though they were not required to take their advice. But in the Magna Carta of 1215 CE the secular and religious magnates forced King John to acknowledge their demands. John, his father, and his brother, Richard the Lion Heart, had increasingly consolidated their power over the barons and the Church. John and his forebears' need for funds to defend French territory they had inherited led John to increase demands for funds from English feudal lords. In the barons' attempts to resist King John's taxes and the imposition of laws with which they disagreed, they demanded that the king win their consent before raising revenues and sending troops anywhere. Animosities increased between 1204 and 1213, but John was at first able to buy off individual lords by granting them feudal titles and land and promising to grant "that the English Church be free, and that the men in our kingdom have and hold all the aforesaid liberties, rights, and concessions well and peaceably, freely and quietly, fully and wholly, for themselves and their heirs, of us and our heirs, in all respects and in all places forever...."[19]

The court magnates, a highly select group of barons, consisted of a relatively small group of people who felt no obligation to extend to commoners the democratic rights they had gained. Even though some scholars believe that laws such as having the punishment fit the crime date at least as far back as the time of King John's father, Henry II, and were even found in town charters of the time, having a written document like the Magna Carta that limited the powers of the king set a precedent that future groups tried to imitate.[20]

From the ancient world to the high Middle Ages, publicizing people's rights on tablets, parchment, or other forms of paper ensured that there would be a written record buttressing future claims for democratic rights. Even when those rights disappeared under subsequent regimes, as most of them did, memories of these written documents lived on or were rediscovered granting legitimacy to those who hoped to create democracies of their own.

CHAPTER 2

Prophetic Movements and Cities of Promise

A medieval German saying claimed that "city air makes you free." The lowest peasant or escaped slave could frequently start a new life, achieve a new identity, and find a certain level of freedom and justice in the city. The process of urbanization—the fact that people lived in cities where they could converse with strangers as well as with neighbors and family members—augmented the possibilities for democracy in sixteenth-century South Asia. The rights to speak, write, and gather with anyone one chose formed the platform on which democracy began to rest. The Sikhs, a religious group founded by Guru Nanak (1469–1539 CE), promoted self-government, caring for the less fortunate, and overcoming the Hindu caste system.[1]

Born a Hindu of the Khartri or Kshatrya caste in the middle of the Punjab near Lahore, Guru Nanak was the son of a tax collector for a local Muslim official. As a boy he showed an early interest in languages and poetry and learned Sanskrit, Persian, Hindi, and Punjabi, the language that was developing in his region. But Guru Nanak's father wanted him to have a "practical" career as a government official, an accountant, a cattle trader, or a shopkeeper, and when the boy was sixteen, his father arranged for him to marry Sulakhni, the daughter of a pious Hindu merchant. The couple had two sons, and Guru Nanak combined his work as a small merchant with intense meditation. Lower-caste Hindus and Bhai Mardana, a Muslim minstrel who became his closest friend, joined Nanak in evening meetings, known as *Sangats*, filled with poetry, songs, and ethical and political discussions. During this period of invasions and religious conflict culminating in the establishment of the Mughal dynasty (1526–1857), Guru Nanak and his companions shared their meals together, violating caste and religious rules. But Guru Nanak carried notions of equality even further

In an effort to overcome social differences in pursuit of holy community, Sikh men gather in a "Sangat" to pray, to listen to scripture in the company of the guru or leader, or simply to serve one another by preparing food, playing music, or listening to stories about the founder, Guru Nanak, and his successors. Gurumustuk Khalsa—Sikhphotos.com

by encouraging marriages among people of different religions and ethnicities. Those who joined him called themselves *Sikhs*, or disciples, but only Bhai Mardana joined him when, following a vision in 1499, Nanak journeyed all over India, including contemporary Pakistan, Bangladesh, and Sri Lanka, and as far west as Mecca, Medina, and Baghdad spreading his religious teachings.[2]

The Hindu Jat people from the northern plain of the Punjab joined Guru Nanak early on in his ministry. They were primarily workers and farmers, who belonged to one of the lower Hindu castes. But, from the tenth century on, their political practices assumed an important role in their identity as a people. A frontier society, prey to conquests from all their neighbors, they lived in fortified villages. In their communities, any adult man who defended the villages was given democratic rights, for example, to elect the five male elders who would govern them, and thus the Jat people incorporated beliefs in equality into their identity as Sikhs.

During Guru Nanak's youth, many Hindus were dissatisfied with elaborate religious rituals, pilgrimages, and conflicting sects that viewed one another with hostility. Some Hindus were attracted to another religious movement called *Bhakti* that emphasized spiritual surrender and recognized the needs of lower-caste people. At the same time Muslims called *Sufis* rejected the formal rituals of their religion. Guru Nanak drew on both Bhakti and Sufi practices to develop congregations that placed the needs of everyday life ahead of the supernatural. Making a commitment to life, for example, Guru Nanak opposed the Hindu practice of *Sati*, the burning of widows alongside their dead husbands. He opposed exorbitant taxes that threw merchants, workers, and farmers into poverty. And he cherished the rule of law that constrained the whims of rulers.

Guru Nanak embraced elements from Islam and Hinduism, but primarily emphasized their most egalitarian characteristics and attempted to reduce their undemocratic qualities. He particularly attacked the Hindu caste system. The Brahmins were the priestly caste that dominated the social and religious hierarchy. But Guru Nanak's caste, the Kshatryas, formed the governing class. Below them on the social scale were the urban artisans who wove and dyed silk and cotton cloth, and those, like the Jat people, who constituted the farmers of the central plain. At the bottom of the heap came the untouchables, originally aboriginals from the mountainous areas and other frontiers of the Indian subcontinent. They worked with leather, collected waste, disposed of garbage, and did the distasteful tasks the society required. Within each caste, women were subordinate to men. The caste system, which placed fixed limitations on people's physical movements from birth to death, paradoxically also assured the separation between political and religious life by keeping Brahmins out of politics. One of the greatest challenges Guru Nanak undertook was his attempt to undermine the caste system.

Guru Nanak also incorporated democratic traditions from Islam, which spread to the Indian subcontinent in the eighth century with the Muslim merchants who settled along its southern and western coasts. The merchants sailed east to Cambodia, Indonesia, and China, carrying dried fruit, nuts, and frankincense to freshen the air in societies that lacked fresh water and efficient waste disposal. The merchants carried back the rich muslin and precious cotton cloth dyed with bright colors that made the area from Lahore to Delhi relatively prosperous. Members of the lower castes in India flocked to the new religion since it opposed the caste system and promoted the equality of all people. As Guru Nanak said "Usurpation of rights of others is forbidden as pork to Muslims and beef to Hindus. The Guru or the *pirs* will come to your rescue only if you shun the carrion of greed."[3]

Guru Nanak attempted to elaborate on democratic traditions in both Hinduism and Islam to reduce the internecine struggles between them, and possibly his most advanced practice was to overcome Hindu and Muslim treatment of women. Guru Nanak invested his sister, his wife, and other women with power in the Sikh congregation. He left the administration of the Sikh community in his wife's hands during the twelve years of his extended travels, and he repeatedly acknowledged women's full participation in the early, pluralist community of the Sikhs.

Developing the concept of a community of equals in the *Sagats*, or congregations, Guru Nanak tried to assure that wherever the early Sikhs gathered, they formed self-governing congregations in which people met together regardless of race or original religion. These congregations functioned as legislatures and as courts that worked out conflicts according to majority rule, and Guru Nanak and the gurus who followed him participated in them as equals. Indeed, as he approached death in 1538, having settled into life as an independent scholar, Guru Nanak handed over leadership of his community to a colleague rather than pass authority to his sons according to hereditary rule. His visionary insights about democracy—his opposition to empty rituals, his insistence on following secular law, and his derision of the caste system that ruined the lives of so many people—held sway for a long time among his followers. The views he promoted continued to prosper through small, decentralized bodies whose actions were reported in the writings of the gurus who followed.

While Guru Nanak attempted to change religious practices to promote the equality of all people, the representatives of the major Castilian cities in faraway Spain vied with their rulers to win representative government and to avoid paying for Spain's rapidly growing empire. As Spain and its empire expanded first through the conquest of Muslim territories in central and southern Spain and then to Africa and the Americas in the late fifteenth and early sixteenth centuries, a substantial portion of the Spanish population continued to live in cities.

King Ferdinand and Queen Isabella, married in 1469 and fought civil wars to establish their legitimacy in various kingdoms that they ruled separately. In 1492 Isabella embarked on a great and finally successful conquest to drive out the King of Granada, the last remaining Muslim monarch in Spain. She expelled the Jews who refused to convert and four years later made the same demand of Muslims. According to legend, she used her personal fortune to finance Christopher Columbus's first voyage to America. To manage her disparate affairs and multiple kingdoms, she organized the Royal Council of Castile made up of trusted barons. She secured archers, foot soldiers, cavalry, and armaments from other barons, but she increasingly depended on the city councils of the virtual 18 city-states of her disparate Castilian kingdoms to pay the taxes that she needed to administer her kingdom. In exchange, the city representatives demanded royal help with the surrounding barons.

When Isabella died in 1504, she had barely begun to establish a systematic pattern of ruling. Since Ferdinand and Isabella ruled separate kingdoms, Isabella's holdings were passed on to their daughter Juana and her husband, Philip the Fair of Flanders (made up of contemporary Belgium, The Netherlands, Luxembourg, and parts of Northern France). Philip's death in 1506 drove his deeply depressed wife Juana into seclusion, and required her father Ferdinand to rule as regent on her behalf until his death in 1516.

Following Ferdinand's death, his sixteen-year-old grandson, Charles V, became king of Castile and Aragon, and Duke of Flanders. Charles, who had always lived in Flanders and spoke no Spanish, appointed a Flemish advisor as regent to head the Royal Council of Castile, and then came to Spain himself in the autumn of 1517. He summoned the *Cortes*, a congress made up of representatives of 18 Castillian cities, to meet him in Valladolid in March 1518. The representatives who consisted of members of the lower aristocracy as well as doctors, lawyers, merchants, and manufacturers reluctantly gave him the funds he demanded, but many delegates resented the bribes and pressure techniques that Charles employed. Angry that Charles had appointed the seventeen-year-old nephew of one of his Flemish advisors as archbishop of Toledo, the highest ecclesiastical position in Spain, they protested against government by someone they regarded as a "foreign" ruler. The city delegates demanded that Charles learn to speak Spanish, marry a Spanish princess, settle in Spain, and rule all his other dominions from there. Most important for the development of democracy, they wanted the Cortes to schedule regular meetings every three years so that the cities could present their grievances when they occurred rather than simply wait until the king needed revenue. Charles promised everything in general and nothing in particular by repeating, "I swear," and quickly left Castile to visit Aragon and Catalonia, the lands he had inherited from Ferdinand.

While Charles was in Barcelona, he learned that his paternal grandfather, Maximilian of Austria, the Holy Roman Emperor and scion of the Hapsburg family, had died in January 1519. Charles immediately sent emissaries to Aachen, Germany, to secure his place as his grandfather's successor. Over the next six months, he borrowed enormous quantities of cash from his German bankers to bribe the electors and hoped to pay them back with revenues from the Castilian city-states.

Even more in need of Castile's contributions from taxes on the wool trade and on money from the American colonies, Charles again called the Cortes to a meeting in March 1520. The delegates, including Juan de Padilla, a member of the lower aristocracy of Toledo, were appalled. They viewed Charles's demands as far exceeding what they were authorized to offer.[4] Under de Padilla's leadership Toledo became a bastion of opposition to taxation without sufficient representation. De Padilla wrote a letter to each of the cities eligible to send representatives to the Cortes inviting them to meet jointly to petition Charles to remain in Spain, stop asking for their support for foreign ventures, and appoint Spaniards to govern them. Although other cities decided to attend the Cortes, Toledo's fear of being forced to pay Charles's bills led them to boycott the meeting.

Other delegates reluctantly voted to grant Charles his revenues and he escaped to Flanders and Germany in May 1520. He left his former tutor the Dutch Adrian of Utrecht, dean of the University of Louvain, and later Pope Adrian VI, to govern Castile, without agreeing to the Cortes's rights to have their grievances heard. The delegates considered Charles's quick exit as proof of his lack of interest in their kingdom and its problems. But, in fact, an uprising defending the rights of the cities

Juan de Padilla, *who appears in this illustration as half armored knight, half urban representative with a feather in his cap, was one of the leaders of the sixteenth century comunero movement that attempted to gain rights for Castilians to initiate legislation, have King Charles V hold regular meetings of the Cortes or parliament, and establish a more just system of taxation. Although defeated and executed in 1521, de Padilla and the comunero movement exemplified early efforts to democratize Spain.* Biblioteca Nacional de España IH/GRUPO/62 to allocate funds in exchange for legislating policy prevented the king from ever collecting the funds he thought he had secured in 1518 and 1520.

Exasperated city delegates met in Ávila in July 1520 and organized themselves into a federation of city councils or *comunidades*, and named Juan de Padilla their leader. The ideas developed in Ávila—the rights to initiate legislation, hold regular meetings of the Cortes, and establish a more regular taxing system—formed the equivalent of Spain's first constitution, and clearly expressed the democratic ideas of some of the new social groups of lower aristocracy as well as physicians, lawyers, and the commercial groups who dominated the city governments. Members of the lower aristocracy, such as de Padilla and his wife María Pacheco, also upheld the interest of the cities against the imperial interests of the king.

María Pacheco, from one of the most powerful aristocratic Christian families of Granada, grew up in the palace of the Alhambra that had been seized from the Muslim King in 1492. She received a classical education, complete with the study of ancient politics. Nevertheless, at fifteen she was forced against her wishes to marry Juan de Padilla, whose family wielded a lot of power in Toledo's city council although they were only members of the lower aristocracy. By law, de Padilla became the sole executor of the considerable fortune Pacheco brought into the marriage. Unlike aristocratic women in Barcelona and elsewhere in Catalonia, Pacheco and other Castilian women lacked control over their own dowries and thus had to depend on the generosity of their husbands for any resources and freedom of movement they themselves enjoyed. By chance, Pacheco's autonomy was considerable.

Juan de Padilla was a gentleman or *hidalgo*, one of those new men and women who fought for equal rights, at least for the lower aristocracy, in early modern Europe. His aged father had defended Toledo's interests against Isabella's encroachments, and the son became a celebrity in his own right as the leader of the urban military forces against Charles V. De Padilla's fame, which seems to have spread by word of mouth, helped him gain a personal following based on his defense of local interests against the barons, who kept trying to confiscate land that belonged to the cities. As in ancient Greece and Rome, the urban poor used common land to feed cattle, hunt, and get firewood, and since the Spanish aristocracy paid no taxes, municipal officials wanted to exclude them from city government. De Padilla was the kind of leader cities like Toledo depended on to protect their interests. A sixteenth-century observer gushed that the people in all the towns opposed to the monarchy loved Juan de Padilla. In fact, he claimed that "Clerics would quit their churches to follow him, women and girls go from village to village to see him, peasants would go with their carts and mules to serve him without pay, soldiers and squires would fight without any wage under his banner, villages where he passed supplied food to him and his troops liberally; when he went through the streets everybody stationed themselves at doors and windows showering on him a thousand blessings, while young boys hailed him with song, calling him 'liberator'."[5]

De Padilla's prominence, lofty as it was, actually derived its power from the vitality of cities such as Ávila, Toledo, Segovia, and Valladolid that were centers of the Spanish wool industry and hotbeds of social change. Santa Teresa of Ávila, who was born in 1515, was only a young child when the *comuneros, the defenders of the comunidades* met. Yet her life exemplifies some of the innovations the comuneros created. She was a local nun from a family that may have converted from Judaism to Catholicism. Like de Padilla and Pacheco, Santa Teresa represented those eager to democratize society at least to include a high degree of local control over daily life free from the interference of the barons and the crown. Arguing that God was among the pots and pans, she organized a new order of nuns, "the barefoot Carmelites," who honored their vows of chastity and poverty and worked in the world outside the convents. People like Santa Teresa depended on the city councils to protect them and poorer groups from the landed nobility and the vagaries of the monarchy.

The comuneros fought from July 1520 through April 1521. Although María Pacheco led the troops from Toledo in defending that city until the following fall, royal troops defeated her husband Juan de Padilla and Juan Bravo of Segovia on April 23, 1521, in the town of Villalar. The king's forces beheaded Juan de Padilla and Juan Bravo, and hung their heads on spikes to warn the population about the price of rebellion. Pacheco, though she escaped death, lived out the rest of her short life in exile in Portugal and died at the age of thirty-six without the amnesty that Charles V had bestowed on almost all the other surviving rebels.

The *comunero* uprising raised perennial questions about democracy. King Charles, eager to pursue his role as an emperor in earnest by imposing a single law and a single set of religious practices over extensive parts of Europe and Latin America, attempted to centralize his power over his dominions and reduce the power of representative institutions such as the Cortes and locally controlled city councils. Had Emperor Charles V been able to forego summoning the Cortes, he would have done so. But he needed the revenues only the cities could provide. The cities, on the other hand, depended on the monarchy for protection against unruly aristocrats.

Ávila's delegates, while claiming to uphold the old laws and traditions, were also developing new social policy as lawmakers frequently do. They wanted the Cortes to meet regularly so that they could initiate laws and gain the king's support and protection against the unruly barons in return for taxes. They gestured toward a form of parliamentary democracy that took hundreds of years to achieve.

Like Guru Nanak and Juan de Padilla and María Pacheco, the English reformers John and Elisabeth Lilburne fought to establish equal justice and freedom from torture as tenets of national law in the early part of the seventeenth century. The Lilburnes challenged the Church of England, the monarchy, Parliament, Puritans, and ultimately Oliver Cromwell, the virtual dictator of England, in their uncompromising insistence on gaining the civil and political rights that have become the bedrock of democracy. The Levellers, the political party John and Elisabeth Lilburne helped launch along with their friends Richard Overton and William Walvyn, were among the earliest groups to express belief in civil as well as political rights. A pamphleteer and a prophet, John Lilburne used his writing to call for trial by jury, the right of a person accused of a crime to confront his or her accusers, rights against self-incrimination, universal male suffrage, freedom of the press, freedom of religion, the end to censorship, abolition of the Monarchy and the House of Lords, annual elections to the House of Commons, term limitations for delegates, and an end to torture as an instrument of government.[6]

John and Elisabeth Lilburne grew up in times of relative economic insecurity. Born in 1615, John Lilburne came from a small landowning family in the north of England, near Durham. His father sent him to London in 1630 to learn the woolen cloth trade. London, like the Spanish, Indian, and Middle Eastern cities of the time, was bustling with commercial activity. Strangers mixed with householders, as they exchanged products and ideas. Indeed, the cities of the world were hotbeds of struggle over individual and collective rights.

The Hapsburgs, the French monarchs, and Henry VIII and his successors on the English throne tried to increase their religious as well as their secular power. In the early sixteenth century, King Henry VIII had broken with the Catholic Church over his wish to divorce Charles V's aunt, Catherine of Aragon, and Henry established the Church of England in which the king and the archbishop of Canterbury replaced the pope as arbiters of religious doctrine. Since the king became the head of the state church, disputes about religious doctrine permeated politics.[7] For instance, the attempt of Protestants to read the Christian Bible and interpret scripture led some of them to dispense with ministers to create a congregation of equals who interpreted scripture for themselves. This communitarian ideal, the notion of a group of equal individuals capable of coming to terms with doctrinal matters, gave many like John Lilburne the sense that matters of the highest import could be decided by individuals reflecting on sacred and profane law.

For rulers like King Henry VIII and Emperor Charles V, religious order dovetailed with maintaining political order, and using torture to maintain the monarchy was no more reprehensible than the Church using torture allegedly to save a person's soul. Some seventeenth-century English radicals like John Lilburne countered by calling for the equality of all to think as they liked, write and publish what they thought, worship without the supervision of priests or ministers, avoid self-incrimination, be free of torture, and generally speak their minds and listen to others who participated in public or in religious centers. Equality before the law, including freedom of speech and rights to publish their ideas, became commitments worth fighting for.

John Lilburne was a popular pamphleteer who promoted the interests of an emerging group of urban artisans, small merchants, and skilled workers who began demanding rights that Lilburne labeled those of freeborn Englishmen. Like many of them, Lilburne put his own body forward in defense of his political ideals. After violating the 1559 law that empowered the Stationers' Guild to confiscate publications that challenged religious doctrine and bring their authors up on charges, the physician John Bastwick and two other activists were arrested for circulating a critique of bishops and other members of the Church of England. The ecclesiastical court, with jurisdiction over them, ordered their ears removed and branded another of the prisoners, William Prynne, on his cheek with an "S" and an "L" for seditious libel.

Lilburne, who had published Bastwick's work in Holland, was also held accountable for distributing incendiary material, and was forced to appear in a secret court known as the Star Chamber. In 1638, when he refused to speak until authorities told him the charges against him and permitted him to confront his accusers, he was tied naked to a cart and beaten as the guards drove him to government headquarters. There he was placed in a wooden frame that held his legs parallel to the ground to shame him and force him to confess to violating the law. When he refused, he was gagged and taken by cart, followed by a crowd of supporters among whom were apprentice artisans, wool workers, the unemployed, pamphleteers, hawkers, and others who walked the city streets. They bore witness to what the torturers were doing to Lilburne and the others and tried to shame them in the court of public opinion. Despite, or even because of their support, Lilburne was taken to prison, where he remained until 1640.

Oliver Cromwell, a member of Parliament, who later became one of the leaders of the English Revolution (1642–51) and then the head of the military government known as the Protectorate (1653–59), helped get Lilburne released. Lilburne immediately joined Cromwell's side in the growing struggle against the king. But Lilburne, loyal to principles rather than people, refused to allow personal relations to interfere with action. Jailed again under Cromwell in 1645 and 1646, he used his time in prison to write more pamphlets and letters railing against those who ignored what he considered democratic rights of free speech and freedom of religious thought.

Like Guru Nanak, Lilburne found supporters among craftsmen and artisans, who promoted hand industry in the cities. He also appealed to urban immigrants, who had their hopes aroused by the political rhetoric of the contending political forces unleashed during the English Revolution. Unlike many of the political activists of the time, Lilburne embraced these new people for whom the old political traditions held no attraction. He organized meetings of apprentices, at which they expressed their anger against their employers, the guild masters, as well as against the government. These apprentices were forced to submit to constraints on their freedom during their long apprenticeships. But their skills in production and trade translated into self-confidence that led them to think that they could generate ideas and turn them into reality. This new generation of men (and some women) believed in the doctrines of equality that Lilburne and others helped formulate.

Lilburne united with many of these progressives when he joined the army as Parliament rose up against the king in the English Revolution. The monarchical forces captured Lilburne outside Oxford and planned to try him for treason. Elisabeth Lilburne, who was pregnant at the time, rode from London to Oxford to get Lilburne freed in an exchange of prisoners. He became a war hero. He resigned from the army when Cromwell instituted a religious oath to the government, which many Quakers and other Protestant denominations refused to take since they believed that swearing to God in secular matters violated the separation of church and state and their religious consciences.

Unable to countenance public discrimination of any kind, Lilburne fulminated against the maintenance of social differences in the Parliamentary army that fought against the king in the revolution. Lilburne's refusal to compromise landed him in prison again in 1647. When he was released in 1648, he and his friends started a newspaper, which they called *The Moderate*. He, Elisabeth Lilburne, Thomas Prince, William Walvyn, and Richard Overton organized a political party, which their enemies labeled "the Levellers," that set about winning civil liberties. Many of its doctrines appeared in their political manifesto, *An Agreement of the People*. "We the free People of *England*," read the *Agreement*, "to whom God hath given hearts, means and opportunity to effect the same . . . Agree to ascertain our Government, to abolish all arbitrary Power, and to set bounds and limits both to our Supreme, and all Subordinate Authority, and remove all known Grievances."[8] In reaction to their radical propositions to reform the system of governance outlined in the *Agreement*, the three men were arrested in the spring of 1649 and, despite the work of Leveller organizer Mary Overton, who succeeded in rousing thousands to sign a petition for their release, the men were imprisoned in the Tower of London, and Lilburne was again accused of treason.

When Lilburne, the Levellers, and other radical democrats called for the abolition of the Monarchy and the House of Lords, Cromwell and his government supported them. But when they demanded universal male suffrage, the Cromwellian government arrested them. Lilburne was far too consistent in his commitments to democracy to keep the support of more opportunistic politicians, or even those willing to work out compromises. Although he thought that he could persuade Cromwell and the Parliament to bring King Charles I to trial, they instead chose to execute the king on their own authority in January 1649 and imprisoned Lilburne for opposing them. The Levellers, with Elisabeth Lilburne again in the lead, organized another petition campaign that engaged over 10,000 angry supporters, especially in London. Despite this support, Cromwell refused to release Lilburne. Again charged with treason, he was imprisoned, tried, exiled, and then exonerated. Between 1649 and 1651, he wrote fewer pamphlets and devoted himself to supporting his family as a soap maker. He returned to attacks on the government for its imperialism in Ireland, England's first colony, and once again was charged with treason. A trial for libel resulted in his banishment to Holland in 1651 on pain of death if he returned. Unable to follow, the beleaguered and abused Elisabeth Lilburne, seven of whose children had died, tried to support their remaining family as a single mother. They were scarcely able to survive.[9]

After a little over two years, in 1653, when Cromwell overthrew Parliament and seized power in a military dictatorship called the Protectorate, John Lilburne audaciously returned to England. Once again brought to trial for his life in July 1653, his apprentice supporters thronged the Guild Hall in London, where he was being tried. In one of the most important trials of the century, Lilburne used his righteous anger to proclaim his rights as a citizen. The jury again proclaimed him not guilty and refused to impose the death penalty. He nevertheless spent the rest of his life in prison. Cromwell moved him around from London to a dungeon in a castle on the Isle of Jersey, and finally to the Dover Tower, from which he was periodically released for home visits. He converted to Quakerism in 1657, shortly before he died at the age of forty-three, leaving Elisabeth Lilburne, herself an activist, to raise their children on her own.

Oddly matched, the efforts of Guru Nanak, María Pacheco, Juan de Padilla, and John and Elisabeth Lilburne actually form a pastiche of how democratic demands for equality and human rights proceeded. When a rich man's steward invited Guru Nanak to a feast with representatives of four Hindu castes, Nanak responded "I belong not to any of the four castes; why am I invited?" The wealthy steward asked why Nanak had snubbed them. Nanak asked both the steward and the poor carpenter at whose house the feast was taking place to bring him a sample of their regular food. As the Sikh legend goes, Nanak then squeezed the carpenter's bread, and milk came out. But when he squeezed the steward's bread, the blood of oppression and bribery came out.[10] Although Nanak made no reference to rights, his preoccupation with justice marked him as someone determined to establish equality. Likewise, de Pacheco, who was from a wealthy family one of whose sons was a viceroy and one of whom was a Catholic bishop, nevertheless could appreciate the need for certain urban groups to gain equality with the emperor and the high aristocracy in determining how resources should be allocated. And the Lilburnes, despite the poverty and repression they endured because of their beliefs, were nevertheless able to stand up against religious and judicial tyranny and demand democratic rights for all.

CHAPTER 3

Democracy against All Odds

Some view democracy simply as representing the act of continuous conversation and deliberation until a consensus is reached. In the eighteenth and early nineteenth centuries, many skilled workers, women of all classes, soldiers, and priests gathered in small societies in order to discuss the political, intellectual, and commercial issues of their day with the goal of creating what we might call democratic governments. Although the concept of "democracy" gained a following among such people, they might well have regarded it as synonymous with mob rule until the committees that participants constructed came into being in the late eighteenth century. If no country or group had a monopoly in taming what could be the wild demands of individuals, democratic practices of talking things through in groups and challenging others to defend their political and intellectual positions regained a standing in the eighteenth century it had not held in centuries, anywhere on earth.

In small-town Boston, whose population never increased much above 15,000 between 1750 and 1770, craftsmen and printers like Paul Revere, who at nineteen had inherited his father's shop and trade as a silversmith while continuing to work as a printer, joined with others who were only willing to consider paying increased government taxes if they had a greater say in how the revenues were spent. While magnates and elite merchants in many medieval cities had long withheld revenues from kings in protest until their demands were met, the eighteenth century went even further as merchants and artisans organized their clubs and enhanced their networks to help shape more productive democratic links between one another.

Revere, who is widely known for his ride in 1775 from Lexington to Concord to alert citizens that British troops were on their way to seize gun powder that the colonial insurgents had stockpiled, is representative of the working people who fought for their rights as citizens and helped define the linkages that would make democracy in the United States possible.[1] Revere grew up in the North End of Boston, along the harbor, among printers, metalworkers, carpenters, rope-makers, shipbuilders, coopers, washerwomen, tailors, and other craftsmen and women. He learned to read and write in a local school and used these skills in his print business. Like later use of social media tools such as Facebook and Twitter, print itself had made possible reducing the political authorities' control over information that was circulating. Print could, of course, be suppressed as the Leveller pamphlets had been, and writers and publishers could be held to account and punished for their views. But even having access to print technology exploded the constraints on democratic and reactionary thought that had previously been circumscribed.

Paul Revere's friend Benjamin Edes was the son of the printer Joseph Edes, who, along with his partner John Gill, began publishing *The Boston Gazette and Country Journal* in 1755. Written largely by workmen like themselves, the *Gazette* and its competitors such as the *Boston Post Boy* provided opportunities for bringing people together to discuss the news of the day. These were the same people who fought on the frontiers and paid taxes as British citizens. These new men and women not only exchanged and commented among friends about the news of the day, but they brought their ideas and their confidence about expressing them into public places where they cajoled and fought their opponents and sought them out in order to exchange ideas and make their own wishes heard. Edes and Gill's other publications included the *North American Almanac* and the *Massachusetts Register*, newspapers that did not actively campaign for one issue or another, but established a notion of a free press as the connective link in a self-governing community.

Printing was all well and good, but information and opinion lies inert if people do not pull it apart through intense commentary. Paul Revere and the artisans, small shopkeepers, and more prosperous people with whom he associated in various grass-roots organizations carried this work out admirably. Grass-roots spread wildly and the associations to which this modern term applies may vary from associations of people who experience shortages and decide to, do something rectify the situation to neighbors who discover that they are victims of environmental hazzards to parents who gather to discuss common problems. The caucuses to which Paul Revere belonged met in Boston's North or South End in casual meetings in inns such as the Green

Dragon Tavern on Union Street where men discussed current political affairs and developed powerful ties to one another. In 1765, some of these caucuses in Boston went further and may have constituted themselves into something closer to an open political club such as the Sons of Liberty that played a large role in the events leading up to the American Revolution.

The start of American Revolution was intimately related to taxation. In order to streamline tax collection and avoid the confrontations involved in taxing merchandise for export, in March 1765, the British government passed the Stamp Act that was to go into effect in November. It would have required nearly all publicly circulating printed matter—all newspapers, pamphlets, almanacs, legal documents, insurance policies, and playing cards—to be printed on paper bearing a stamp paid for in advance. Designed to avoid the incessant pursuit of smugglers that led authorities to invade warehouses and private homes, the tax effectively burdened all legal and commercial traffic, intensifying the threat of economic collapse. The increased taxes the British, French, Spanish, Portuguese, and Dutch imposed on their colonies in the eighteenth century antagonized virtually all colonized people, and sometimes united groups who otherwise had no common identity. In fact, while attempting to simplify tax collection, the Stamp Act of 1765 created a community of patriots opposed to British imperialism. Resistance to this hated imposition of an outside authority generated local assemblies that regarded taxation as a local matter over which their own provincial assemblies should have ultimate control. Nine colonies sent delegates to a Stamp Act Congress in New York in October 1765 that issued a protest against taxation without representation, arguing "that it is inseparably essential to the freedom of a people, and the undoubted right of Englishmen, that no taxes be imposed on them, but with their own consent, given personally, or by their representatives . . ." They went on to add "that the only representatives of the people of these colonies, are persons chosen therein by themselves, and that no taxes ever have been, or can be constitutionally imposed on them, but by their respective legislatures."[2] The Stamp Act was repealed in March 1776.

The victory of these locally controlled representative institutions that promoted material as well as abstract benefits heightened the resolve that popular institutions, rather than Parliamentary decrees, should govern the colonies. In the context of continued conversations about freeborn Englishmen and their rights (reminiscent of the Levellers' demands), colonists questioned whether they were or should be subordinate to fellow citizens who lived across the Atlantic. By the mid-eighteenth century, colonists had established their own routines for feeding, clothing, housing, and governing themselves, and any interruption in these routines was bound to cause havoc. Yet the British were attempting to centralize power and needed increased revenue to do it. Parliament, trying to recoup its losses from the French and Indian Wars, turned again and again to the American settlers for economic support, with the Stamp Act of 1765, the equally notorious Townshend Duties in 1767, and eventually a tax on tea.

The Massachusetts Assembly, which represented local white male property holders, had appointed and paid local judges until 1773. In that year, Parliament decided to take control of the local judiciary and imposed the infamous tax on tea to pay the judges' wages. Not only were the British reducing the colonists' powers, but they were making them pay for their diminished control. In order to enhance their own authority, local leaders in Massachusetts formed so-called Committees of Correspondence and Safety that served as mini-legislative bodies, and Sam Adams helped organize eighty such Committees throughout Massachusetts. Settlers in other colonies followed suit and in 1773 the Virginia House of Burgesses appointed its own province-wide Committee of Correspondence.

If democracy entailed public debate, news was its currency. It took several months for the colonists to learn that Parliament had passed the Tea Act in May 1773. When the first of four ships destined for Boston arrived on November 28, 1773, Governor Thomas Hutchinson, unlike the governors in New York, Philadelphia, and Charleston, accepted the delivery, thus provoking local people to take action. As the tea was being unloaded on December 16, 1773, a now famous group of determined citizens probably organized by Sam Adams took matters into their own hands. More than a hundred men, a few sporting Indian headdress, dumped the tea chests into Boston harbor in a powerful act of resistance, a Tea Party, against what was widely considered British tyranny.

Many local women, with significant economic power as controllers of household economies, joined Sam Adams in a boycott of English goods. The practice of boycotting, thought to have emerged among Irish tenant farmers in the eighteenth century, became an early form of passive resistance that democratic groups around the world have employed to promote their own interests against more powerful adversaries. When the British, recognizing the popular power of the boycott, retaliated by placing the city of Boston under virtual martial law

One of the ablest and most dedicated community organizers in the American Revolution, Samuel Adams helped launch the Committees of Correspondence that formed the basis for the Constitutional Congress. A person of virtue who committed his life to the benefit of others, he wrote in a 1748 essay, "It is not unfrequent to hear men declaim loudly upon liberty, who, if we may judge by the whole tenor of their actions, mean nothing else by it but their own liberty—to oppress without control or the restraint of laws all who are poorer or weaker than themselves."
Library of Congress
LC-USZ62-45248

SAMUEL ADAMS Efq.
One of the DELEGATES *from the Province of* MASSACHUSETTS-BAY
to the General Continental CONGRESS *of* NORTH-AMERICA.

closing down the port, local citizens refused to serve on juries for the duration of British rule. Philadelphia, in solidarity with Boston, called a Continental Congress at Carpenters' Hall in 1774 and delegates drew up a list of grievances. Other local committees also went to work listing their demands, and, from them, Dr. Joseph Warren wrote up the Suffolk Resolves, the precursor to the Declaration of Independence. Along with the Fairfax Resolves of Virginia, the Suffolk Resolves called for popular control over military and civilian issues. The king refused to accept these demands, and, within a year, on July 3, 1776, the Continental Congress met again and issued the Declaration of Independence, thus launching the American Revolution.

This well-known sequence of events highlights how direct democratic practices often undergird representative democracy. The American colonists sought rights that lower-middle-class and working-class people in England, Scotland, and Ireland lacked until the end of the nineteenth century. As late as 1819, following the Napoleonic wars, English crowds peacefully gathered in Peter's Field outside Manchester to demand some of the rights of self-government that propertied white American men had achieved through the American Revolution. It took the 1832 Reform Act and the Chartist Movement of 1838 to 1848 and finally the 1867 and 1884 Reform acts for British working-class men (but not yet women) to gain universal suffrage even if they lacked property, a pattern largely repeated in the United States. The much applauded ability of the American colonists to form democratic institutions and to create a sense of a public good set a precedent that even they themselves opposed spreading. They did not, for example, include indigenous people (who, like the Iroquois, had their own government long houses), free women, indentured servants, or slaves in the public good that they promoted in the Constitution that was passed in 1789.

A common trait of democratic movements worldwide is participants' demand for inclusion in decision-making. Even those who lack access to public forums because of their sex, race, or ethnicity, who lack leisure to organize and mobilize frequently, lack meeting places and even the paper on which to print news, proclamations, or posters, periodically join grass-roots movements and attempt through them to form stable democratic organizations. This was especially evident during the French Revolution and democratic uprisings in late eighteenth-century Brazil.

In 1789, the high price of bread and the failure of the French Crown to secure sufficient revenues to meet the economic and social needs of the country forced the king to call together the Estates General, the governing body made up of wealthy urban merchants, aristocrats, and Church leaders. Despite the multiple social groups assembled, only the merchants and professionals, who made up the Third Estate, could be asked to provide revenues, as Juan de Padilla and members of the other sixteenth-century Castilian towns had been required to do. The representatives of the three French estates, aristocracy, clergy, and the merchants and property owners of the Third Estate, met separately in the late spring of 1789, and, when the groups seemed incapable of resolving the financial crisis, the Third Estate declared itself a Constituent Assembly. Outside the official meetings, groups of ordinary Parisian women, unable to afford food, mobilized as they had previously done, to demand bread at what they considered a just price. Some working-class women joined male relatives in burning down the hated Bastille prison in the heart of the popular district of Paris, thus releasing political prisoners and debtors as well as ordinary criminals. Their attack on July 14, 1789, launched the French Revolution, which, like the American Revolution, created more aspirations for popular democracy than it was able to satisfy.

Even before the revolution took place, slavery and women's absence from government bodies was cause for consternation of some groups, and Olympe de Gouges, a poor playwright, activist, and incipient feminist, spoke out against the marginalization of women and slaves. De Gouges, who was not interested in waiting for change, was determined to do away with privileges associated with gender, race, and class. She focused on creating a democratic society in which descendants of African slaves and all women could be full citizens. Even before the French Revolution began in 1789, those supporting slavery in the French Caribbean castigated her play "Zamore and Mirzrah or Black Slavery" (*Zamore et Mizrah, ou l'esclavage des nègres*), written in 1783 and published in 1786, and her essay "Reflections on Black People" (*Réflexions sur les hommes nègres*), which many thought was far too outrageous to circulate.[3]

Faced with a government that meant "men" when it used that noun, many women and abolitionists recognized that the Declaration of the Rights of Man and Citizen passed by the National Assembly in 1789 excluded women and slaves. Both Olympe de Gouges and the English governess and political critic Mary Wollstonecraft, who was then living in Paris, responded in forceful ways, insisting on women's rights to participate equally in the public sphere. De Gouges retaliated against the exclusion of women by writing "The Declaration of the Rights of Women" in 1791. In Article II, she wrote that "political rights should include the natural rights of all men and women. These rights are liberty, property, security, and especially resistance to oppression."[4] When the slave uprising led by Toussaint l'Ouverture ensued in 1791 in Haiti, France's most lucrative colony, abolitionists like de Gouges were unfairly blamed for the violence, as American abolitionists such as William Lloyd Garrison would be at the time of Nat Turner's slave rebellion in 1831. But in each case, slave holders not abolitionists or slaves should be held accountable.

In free societies, attempts to balance collective and individual rights became a central preoccupation of democratic movements from the eighteenth century on. Between 1789 and 1793, women of all classes assembled in public places in Paris to argue about how the government should proceed. The aristocratic Dutch immigrant Etta Palm d'Aelders organized the Patriotic and Beneficent Society of Female Friends of Truth in 1791 and hoped to generate programs to train young women to be seamstresses and skilled workers. She and other middle-class activists formed patriotic societies and promoted divorce legislation through coordinated action with other women's clubs.[5]

The clubs helped generate proposals in each of the districts of Paris. As early as 1791 "The Fraternal Society of Patriots of Both Sexes Defenders of the Constitution," a mixed-sex group that reserved two leadership positions for women, formed in Paris. They joined some of Paris' poorest men and women in the galleries of the male Cordeliers and Jacobin political clubs and helped form a "Central Committee of Parisian Fraternal Societies" in May 1791. When King Louis XVI, unwilling to cooperate with the National Assembly in governing the country, fled Paris, the Central Committee called for the establishment of a republic and organized a mass public petition-signing demonstration at the Champ-de-Mars in Paris on July 17, 1791. The Marquise de Lafayette, who had given such strong support to the American patriots against Britain, willingly followed the National Assembly's orders and sent in troops to repress the petitioners, ultimately killing fifty people. Those believed to have participated in the demonstration were hunted down, and their clubs were closed for two weeks following the massacre. When Austria attacked France on April 20, 1792 in hope of restoring the absolutist monarchy, Louis XVI, the brother-in-law of the Austrian emperor, made only feeble attempts to defend the country, thus leaving local citizens to defend themselves.[6]

During the spring and summer of 1792, delegates from the forty-eight neighborhoods of Paris created a popular congress made up of men and women who discussed matters ranging from local administration to how to shape a new state. Taking participatory democracy seriously, they organized garbage collection and formed police battalions. Later, as fears of invasion intensified, they generated surveillance committees. They pondered local, regional, and national need, and relayed their opinions to the successive legislatures: the Constituent Assembly, the Legislative Assembly, and finally the National Convention, which declared a republic in late September 1792. Whole families, their boarders, and women inside and outside their clubs participated in the nightly debates in the local general assemblies, spreading the news, partly derived from hearsay and rumor, partly from radical newspapers and pamphlets written and published by radical journalists.

In 1793, as anxiety about imminent foreign invasions and counter-revolutionary activity increased, the need for security also led to repression of dissent. On one hand, the clubs and general assemblies in the local districts continued to meet, but fear of subversion increasingly made reasoned argument and honest disputes more difficult to pursue. Women, who ranged from those who took in washing to those who did piecework at home, to servants who lived on their own, to skilled workers, teachers, and midwives, joined in the discussions in cheap cafes. There, for the price of one drink, they could argue about the news as reported in the radical press and effectively join in commentary about the articles that were read aloud.

Radical women like the actress Louise Lacombe and the chocolate maker Pauline Léon pursued an even more innovative course. In 1793, they organized the single-sex Society of Revolutionary Republican Women and welcomed working-class women to join in.

Under the pressures of the revolution, many of those in the Society of Revolutionary Republican Women became increasingly violent in their rhetoric and denounced anyone who opposed them. Their list of enemies ranged from the market women of Les Halles, who had helped lead the street action that succeeded in launching the revolution, to the increasingly hated Girondin Party, made up of largely middle-class representatives, whose alleged moderation seemed to threaten the republic. When Girondin supporter Charlotte Corday assassinated the radical journalist Jean-Paul Marat in July 1793, many of the fears of the radical women were realized, and they increasingly called for tighter security and suppression of moderates, including the Girondins.

Helping to drive the Girondins from power, the Society of Revolutionary Republican Women, the working-class washerwomen whose livelihoods were constantly under the threat of rising soap prices, and numerous poor women who endured the fluctuating price of bread continued to make extra-parliamentary claims on politicians. Aching to make their ideas known, women from the Society joined municipal government meetings during the day and clubs and societies at night in 1793. And, as the central government cracked down on popular meetings and limited assemblies to twice a month, the local people reorganized as clubs, causing at least one woman to remark that they would have been "very aggravated if we had to miss the popular assembly even just once. At least there we improve our knowledge."[7] When, in October 1793, women were excluded from belonging to the clubs, they participated from the sidelines. For the next two years, as

The Society of Revolutionary Republican Women, one of the more radical of the many political clubs and associations that functioned during the French Revolution, was unique in that it was open exclusively to women. Although its members were committed to maintaining order in their own proceedings, they often verbally attacked less radical delegates to the National Convention, and acted as vigilantes against anybody they thought was hoarding supplies or price gouging. Musée de la Ville de Paris, Musée Carnavalet, Paris. Erich Lessing / Art Resource, NY

most assemblies were suppressed, these clubs were the only popular political centers to remain open. Without any certified political rights, seamstresses and unemployed women, washerwomen, and women peddlers moved around from meeting to meeting, exercising their rights to create a popular democracy that existed only when they practiced it.

The American and French Revolutions, with all their faults and shortcomings, raised the possibilities for wider participation in democratic decision-making, a potential that was not lost on people in Latin America. In Brazil, which represents fully half the land area of the continent, democratic aspirations emerged before and after the revolutions in the United States and France. Enhanced by Free Masons and guild-like *confradias*, associations dedicated to the worship of special saints and madonnas, artisans of different races organized to gain more power over their daily lives through democratic political transformations. Two uprisings demonstrate desires for widespread democratic changes: The Mining Conspiracy (or *Inconfidência Mineira*) of 1788 and 1789 in Vila Rica de Ouro Preto, in Minas Gerais northwest of Rio de Janeiro, and the 1798 Tailors' Conspiracy, led by mulattos or mixed-race people in the northeastern city of Salvador do Bahia. Though very different, each of these programs for change point to a political theory in formation, some elements referring to improving economic conditions and others to interpretations of freedom. In Minas Gerais in 1788 and 1789, a group came together through various friendship networks and possible social ties. It was made up of local businessmen, mine operators, a soldier passed over for promotion, a poet and intellectual, several priests, some landowners, and a group of tax collectors who could not afford to pay the revenues for which they were responsible. They hatched a plan known as "the Conspiracy of the Province of Minas Gerais" to create a democratic republic in their home region. Some of the conspirators, including the priests, were influenced by their extremely liberal educations at the University of Coimbra in Portugal. They seemingly wanted to create a democratic country divided into municipal assemblies and a national legislative body that would share authority with a head of state who would hold office for only one year. They must have imagined threats from other regions or from the Portuguese government itself since the revolutionaries planned to form a national militia for protection.[8] Their rather moderate demands were for a university, since none existed in Brazil, and a legislature made up of local male leaders familiar with local economic and social conditions in the country. But they never really grappled with what such a regional government would mean for the nation as a whole.

In the late seventeenth century, massive gold reserves had been discovered in the Brazilian province of Minas Gerais, close to the mountainous town of Vila Rica de Ouro Preto. The gold first appeared as dust in the rivers and then as veins in mining shafts that from the late seventeenth to the mid-eighteenth centuries yielded a huge proportion of the gold reserves appropriated by European governments. The Portuguese, who dominated the slave trade and had already brought huge numbers of slaves to the sugar plantations of northeastern Brazil, transported more Africans, largely from the Portuguese colony of Angola, to work in the mines. Seeking slaves of short stature who could allegedly stand up in the low mining shafts, the mine owners—knowing the relative ease of importing more slaves—literally worked the miners to death. Although the rich veins lasted only for half a century or so, the mines created financial fortunes for their owners and delivered twenty percent of the wealth of the Portuguese Crown. But as profits declined in the mid-eighteenth century, the Marquês de Pombal, prime minister of Portugal, attributed declining revenues to recalcitrant tax-payers and demanded a fixed tax rather than a percentage of production. This threatened the financial survival of many of the businessmen who were deeply in debt. Seeking greater revenues, Pombal confiscated church tithes, leaving churches, the poor, and even the clergy destitute. The poverty and insecurity of the church may be one reason several priests decided to join the plot. At the last moment, the Crown cancelled the tax and averted the uprising. But just before this occurred, one of the conspirators denounced the poet, various businessmen, and several priests. The *alferes* or second lieutenant Joaquim José da Silva Xavier, a career soldier and part-time dentist, known as *Tiradentes* (or tooth-puller), was the poorest of the conspirators, and he ultimately took responsibility for the scheme. Often passed over for promotion because he lacked family connections, his ties to elite co-conspirators seems to have had less to do with social aspirations than with hopes for creating a more comprehensive political system that would unite

Tiradentes (Joaquim José da Silva Xavier), one of the leaders of the 1789 republican uprising in Brazil, faces the authorities as they come to arrest him. Attracted by the ideals they associated with the constitution of the United States, Tiradentes and his co-conspirators also rejected having their town of Ouro Preto pay inflated taxes far in excess of the profits local mines were producing. Acervo do Museu Júlio de Castilhos

people of all classes and emancipate Black and mulatto slaves born on the continent.[9]

The Inconfidência Mineira Conspiracy differed from the American Revolution since few of its activists engaged in local self-governing assemblies and few, if any miners and artisans, let alone mulattos or freed slaves, were directly involved. The Tailors' Conspiracy (*Conjuraçao dos Alfaiates*) that occurred in the northeastern port city of Salvador in 1798 was, however, led by mulattos such as the tailor João de Deus do Nascimento. The plantations surrounding Salvador produced the sugar, indigo, and cotton, which, unlike the mines, were increasingly prosperous at the end of the eighteenth century.

One day in mid-August 1798, twelve posters calling for the creation of a republic mysteriously appeared on church walls. The open call to arms of approximately 200 alleged conspirators was designed to turn the streets into centers of mobilization. The ten percent of the population who could read would presumably talk to those who were illiterate in order to win their support. The posters promised equality of all people, pay raises for those serving in the military and militias, free trade, and price reduction on staple products such as meat and manioc.[10] The Tailor's Conspiracy engaged at least a few women, low-ranking soldiers, artisans, a school teacher, local intellectuals who, though poor, owned over one hundred books, and mulatto tailors like João de Deus do Nascimento. And, in a city where only one-third of the population was white, the group promised to free all slaves.

A general meeting on August 25, 1798, in the Dique Field just outside Bahia attracted only fourteen of the approximately 200 thought to be actively involved in planning the uprising. The authorities moved in quickly and arrested those they marked as leaders. The degree of repression imposed on alleged conspirators ranged from incarceration, whippings, and abandonment off the coast of Africa to hangings after which the bodies were drawn and quartered. The swift repression seems to demonstrate the depth of fear over the uprising of the largely Black and mulatto population.[11]

The existence of slavery in so many of the countries that underwent democratic revolutions raises perennial questions about the limits of democratic commitment in the age of democratic revolutions. While Thomas Jefferson accepted the existence of slavery in his version of democracy, the late eighteenth-century democratic movements in Brazil were made up of mulatto and Black freedmen and slaves and attempted, as in the Mineira Conspiracy, to make provision for freeing slaves born in Brazil.

Other slaves and freedmen and women of color were able to organize democratically in Brazil through associations connected with the Catholic Church. Throughout Minas Gerais, but especially in Ouro Preto, the wealthy invested in church building and decoration, and the poor and middling groups, including slave and free blacks and mulattos, formed benefit societies tied to different religious groups. These societies not only accumulated resources equivalent to life-insurance policies to cover funerals for themselves and their families, but also served as discussion and pressure groups to help slaves and freedmen and women express their wishes. In Vila Rica de Ouro Preto, the architect and sculptor known as Aleijadinho became head of the confraternity of mulattos dedicated to promoting the worship of St. Joseph (São José), who, as a carpenter, was sometimes adopted as the patron saint of workers. Particular madonnas and saints such as the Virgin of the Rosary and the only Black female saint, St. Ephigenia of the Cross, for whose cult Aleijadinho constructed a chapel, were also thought to be especially attentive to the needs of Blacks and mulattos.[12]

Independent groups of citizens mobilized in the American, French, and Brazilian democratic movements, sometimes working through preexisting societies such as the Free Masons. In France, democratic revolutionaries formed political clubs and local legislative committees that sometimes included women, and in Brazil, similar groups were run by or included Blacks and mulattos. They gathered together and tried to create the embryos of future popular democratic governments. In the course of their struggles, American colonists created a democratic republic that reinvigorated existing charters, laws, and institutions and created new ones. Yet, as became clear in the *Federalist Papers*, especially in the works by James Madison, the American patriotic leaders were perennially afraid of the masses they associated with mob violence. As Madison expressed in *Federalist Paper No. 10*, "Measures are too often decided, not according to the rules of justice and the rights of the minor party, but by the superior force of an interested and overbearing majority."[13] Underscoring this same preoccupation with a suspicion of majority rule, he wrote in *Federalist Paper No. 48*, "One hundred and seventy-three despots would surely be as oppressive as one."[14] And the white men who succeeded in creating an independent country, remembered neither its women nor its slaves.

In France, artisans and workers, including women, helped launch the revolution through political organization and perpetual conversation. In their local assemblies based in their own neighborhoods, they created loose organizations with tight bonds. That is, they transformed their clubs, workshops, and taverns into centers of debate and legislation, converting themselves into citizens of popular democracies. They advanced their ideas through public debate with their neighbors and political allies, but they could not consistently maintain local democratic assemblies and clubs.

In Brazil, with the courts closed to all but the elite, groups like the religious brother- and sisterhoods contributed to providing people with an organizational structure to fight for democratic changes. Not yet having even those local institutions or a relatively free press that would enable them to relay their views in a peaceful fashion to fellow citizens or those in charge of the national government, those committed to social change in eighteenth-century Brazil were forced to express themselves almost exclusively through attempted uprisings. But, despite the revolutionary violence of the eighteenth century, local citizens generated independent institutions that shaped all subsequent struggles for democracy.

CHAPTER 4

Which People Shall Rule?

In Western Europe and the Americas, a popular press, the lifeblood of any democratic government, proliferated in the late eighteenth century where political writings were read aloud in cafes, bars, coffeehouses, and political clubs. By the time the French Revolution began in 1789, there were over 500 newspapers in Paris alone. Often enough, from 1796 to 1815, the hero and villain of these late eighteenth and early nineteenth-century news reports was Napoleon Bonaparte. Between 1796 and 1804, the man who had grown up in Corsica and attended French military schools went from being an unknown and relatively inexperienced young general fighting in northern Italy to becoming the Emperor of France. One thing that helped him make his name and solidify his power was his early recognition of the importance and utility of printed newsletters and newspaper articles. As he reminded his troops in a motivational proclamation distributed to them in 1796, "You have won battles without cannon, crossed rivers without bridges, made forced marches without shoes, camped without brandy and often without bread . . . only republican troops could have endured what you have endured."[1]

With the wealth Napoleon gained as a result of booty he collected on military campaigns as Commander of the French Army in Italy, he financed two newspapers directed largely at his troops, and used them as sounding boards:[2] "All of you are consumed with a desire to extend the glory of the French people; all of you long to humiliate those arrogant kings who dare to contemplate placing us in fetters; all of you desire to dictate a glorious peace, one which will indemnify the Patrie [Fatherland] . . .; all of you wish to be able to say with pride as you return to your villages, 'I was with the victorious army of Italy!'"[3] Realizing that war was not limited to the battlefield and that "four hostile newspapers are more to be feared than a thousand bayonets,"[4] he extolled his own virtues and promised his troops to lead them "into the most fertile plains in the world. Rich provinces, great cities will be in your power. There you will find honor, glory and riches."[5] Using his reputation as a general and his political alliances in Paris, he overthrew the Republic in 1799 and he became the dictator and then the Emperor of France, taking care to control the press at home and in all the countries that he subsequently conquered.

When Napoleon conquered Spain and put his own brother on the throne in 1808, he was probably unaware of existing multiracial democratic movements in Spain's Latin American colonies. The invasion of Spain launched three separate but interlocking democratic movements. In the absence of the King who had been forced to abdicate, former Spanish advisors, aristocrats, members of the military, and representatives from Spanish cities gathered to form a government of their own. In 1810, this ill-defined group joined by various representatives from Latin America organized a Cortes and began writing a liberal constitution that was completed in 1812. The constitution established a representative government, reformed the tax system, created a civil service, and, most importantly, established a free press and the ideal of equality before the law for themselves and their colonies.

Across the Atlantic and the Pacific, local Spanish officials continued to demand their right to rule Spain's colonies in Latin America and the Philippines. But even prior to the Napoleonic invasion of Spain, local landowners and merchants in Spanish America had been attempting to replace the Spanish authorities with their own governing committees or *juntas*, and indigenous people and those of African descent had attempted to secure more rights for themselves. Members of both groups argued that Bonaparte's seizure of power severed any remaining ties between Spain and its colonies. For example, in 1810, the Mexican priest Father Miguel Hidalgo joined indigenous people in the area surrounding the town of Dolores and called for outright independence from Spain and the abolition of slavery. Although Hidalgo was soon captured and executed in 1811 by the Spanish authorities, the struggle he began to wage continued. Another local Mexican priest, the Afro-Mestizo, José María Morelos, assumed Hidalgo's mantle and reiterated his call for the abolition of slavery, an end to racial and class distinctions, and free elections for all male citizens. Demanding the confiscation of property of all those who remained loyal to Spain, Morelos excoriated "the wealthy nobles and the employees of the ruling elite . . . who are the enemies of the nation and the adherents of tyranny."[6] To turn the tide, he helped launch a constitutional congress in 1813 that created a constitution the following year. But Morelos's

In 1810 in the town of Dolores, Father Miguel Hidalgo calls for Mexico's independence from Spain, thus launching a wave of revolutions that by 1825 freed most of Spain's Latin American colonies. The painting by Juan O'Gorman, which hangs in Mexico City's National Historical Museum, shows Hidalgo leading indigenous people, peasant farmers, and many of Mexico's most prominent nineteenth-century political leaders all assembled under the banner of the Virgin of Guadalupe, the mestiza Madonna. Although no one recorded Hidalgo's revolutionary proclamation on September 16, 1810, he is often quoted as saying, "Long live Our Lady of Guadalupe! Death to bad government!" The Granger Collection, New York assassination in 1815 precluded the reforms he helped shape from coming to fruition. By midcentury, a liberal government headed by Benito Juárez was among the first governments to grant universal male suffrage, although for many years rigged elections robbed the franchise of its significance.

The final defeat of Napoleon by the combined forces of Britain, Prussia, Austria, and Russia and the re-imposition of a reactionary order through the Congress of Vienna in 1815 attempted to crush any democratic reforms that had been instituted since 1789. But even the repressive force unleashed by reactionaries led by the Russian Tsar Alexander I and the Chancellor of the Austrian Empire Prince Klemens von Metternich could not entirely crush the secret societies and revolutionary groups burrowing beneath the surface.

One of the unlikely sources of democratic ideals came from young Russian aristocratic veterans of the war against Napoleon. Many young Russian officers sent to enforce the tsar's reactionary policies became conscious of disparities between Western Europe and their homeland and embraced the democratic goals of the French and American revolutions. Pavel Pestel, who had been educated in Dresden, had been influenced by egalitarian goals that he identified with the French Revolution. In his study *Russian Truth* (*Russkaya Pravda*), Pestel argued for the abolition of feudalism and the end to the class system that sentenced serfs (feudal peasants) to be permanently tied to the land on which they were born. Instead, he wanted to abolish serfdom and nationalize the land so that the state could achieve "the greatest possible happiness of the greatest number."[7] These rather schematic ideas became a preliminary program for the transformation of Russia that Pestel and several other radical officers attempted to put into action.

These young men set out to reform Russia along the lines of improvements they had seen in the West. The Northern Society, first organized in 1822 in St. Petersburg and Moscow under the leadership of Suroji Muraev, began plotting the overthrow of the Tsar and the establishment of freedom of the press and religion, the abolition of serfdom, an end to the draft, reform of the courts, and the creation of city, district, provincial, and regional governments that would be run by elected officials.[8]

On December 14, 1825, about one thousand Russian army officers, many of them belonging to the poorer nobility and affiliated with the Northern Society, rose up in St. Petersburg, and refused to swear allegiance to the new Tsar Nicholas I. Easily captured, Pestel, Muraev, and three others viewed as leaders were tried and executed while hundreds of others were sent to endure harsh exiles in Siberia. But the "Decembrists," as they came to be known, became role models for those who wanted to democratize Russia where a large part of the population lived as serfs under feudal conditions. Rejecting the rule of the Tsar and his advisors, the Decembrists became increasingly committed to the individual on one hand and the destiny of the nation on the other.[9]

The Decembrists were not the only forces seeking to democratize their nations. Following the demise of Napoleon in 1815, the reinstitution of conservative governments had forced many democratic movements underground into secret societies such as the Masonically based Carbonari in Italy. Other popular groups, made up of artisans and small manufacturers, formed utopian communes in France, Spain, Italy, Great Britain, and the United States where they produced agricultural and manufactured goods. Others joined together in democratic trade unions to provide the masses of workers with the means to decide how production would be organized.

British workers, who lacked representation in Parliament, resumed demands first made by the Levellers in the seventeenth century and organized the first mass movement in Europe. The Chartists—known for The People's Charter (a direct evocation of the Magna Carta), drawn up by thirty-eight-year-old cabinetmaker William Lovett for the London National Workingmen's Association in 1838—attempted to win universal male suffrage, the secret ballot, annual Parliaments, open elections to Parliament and salaries for delegates, along with the right to form unions. For over ten years, the Chartists held rallies and mass demonstrations widely publicized in the press to draw mostly working-class men and women into the struggle. Despite their organizational abilities and the three petitions they submitted to the House of Commons, their successes lay only in the precedents they set. The petitions themselves faced ridicule and rejection although the first charter had hundreds of thousands of signatures and the third, submitted in 1842, contained nearly three million signatures. Despite its failures, the Chartist movement may have been the most important working-class movement before the great early twentieth-century revolutionary workers' movement in Russia.[10]

Worldwide economic crises, the result of geographical expansion, financial speculation, bad harvests, and high food prices in the middle of the nineteenth century, increased a sense of instability across many continents. But at the same time, uprisings and reform movements swept the globe and demonstrated a sense of a shared destiny and greater belief in the potential for collective achievement than had ever been possible earlier in history. Artisans, craftsmen, laborers, students, politicians, artists, and intellectuals, including women, began to seek democratic control over their own lives and over their governments. The sense that ordinary people could collectively govern themselves emerged in a variety of settings and quickly became associated with ideals of direct and representative democracy in the service of nationalism.

In 1843, for example, the Italian musician and patriot, Giuseppe Verdi, composed the opera *I Lombardi* that focused on how the medieval commune of the Lombards in Milan rose up and defeated the medieval Holy Roman Emperor Frederick Barbarossa. As a defense of Milanese and Venetian independence from Austrian domination and as an exhortation to create an independent Italian state, the opera represented a strong rebuke to the contemporary Austrian rulers who depended on Italy for one-third of its financial revenues.[11] Verdi's eagerness to have the opera performed in France at the end of 1847, just before the February Revolution in France and the Italian uprisings against the Austrians in Milan and Venice in March, was a direct attempt to use his music for political purposes. Austrian censorship of performances of this opera, and, more importantly, Austria's continued domination of Northern Italy until 1859 and its control over the province of Venice until 1866 inhibited the formation of the Italian state.[12]

Once again, France led the way in attempting radical changes and suffering widespread repression. On February 22, 1848, crowds in Paris demanded an end to the July Monarchy of Louis-Phillip of Orleans and its replacement with a republic, by which they meant little more than a monarchy without a king. Crowds of working- and middle-class women, craftspeople, and students demanded and sometimes gained civil and political rights, including universal male suffrage and constitutional governments, although French women did not get the vote until 1944.

Nothing contributed to the spread of revolution in 1848–49 more than the proliferation of newspapers. Newspapers widely disseminated in cafes, bars, coffeehouses, and clandestine political clubs in nearby countries energized dissidents and provided them with their own platforms for debate. And press freedom improved immediately after the various uprisings ensued. By 1849 there were 450 different newspapers sold in Paris alone, while the number of issues distributed daily went from 50,000 to 400,000. With the uprisings of 1848 in Rome, Venice, and Vienna, the number of newspapers also proliferated, and their primary concern was the demand for constitutional government.[13]

Five days after the initial uprising in Paris in February, democrats consisting largely of middle-class professionals in Baden, Germany, rose up and demanded press freedom, jury trials, and the creation of a parliament. The German states, ruled largely by individual kings and dukes, mostly gave in to liberal reforms. In Vienna, university students seized the initiative supported by a radical professor of theology. The students congregated in the university's largest hall and drew up a petition calling for free elections, and the rector of the university agreed to present their demands to the emperor Ferdinand. Prior to 1848, students in Milan and Prague who had expressed hopes for reform had been immediately drafted into the army and forced to do heavy labor, but in 1848 the Viennese students were initially successful in their pursuit of democratic change. When unemployed workers joined the students, it appeared as if a revolution might take place. The army hesitated to attack the students and workers, and the emperor called off the troops when some bloodshed did occur. He turned over arms to the students and workers, declared freedom of the press, and promised far-reaching government reforms.[14] Shortly thereafter, the reactionary state chancellor and foreign minister, Prince Klemens von Metternich, who had famously said that "when France sneezes, Europe catches a cold," was forced into exile to the great joy of the urban crowds. While liberals took their time hammering out a constitution, perhaps as a delaying tactic, popular support for the students and workers diminished over the late spring and summer. The emperor and his family held on until the military was able to return from campaigns in Italy and elsewhere to crush the revolution in Vienna.

In fact, democratic movements were suppressed all over Europe. In April 1848, when the British Chartists renewed their efforts to win universal male suffrage, they were defeated by the government's enormous show of force. Although moderate constitutional governments were installed elsewhere in Europe, the more radical populist Chartists had to wait more than thirty years to achieve their goal of universal male suffrage and nearly a half-century more for suffragists to win votes for women in Great Britain and Ireland. The series of movements that made 1848 a watchword for democratic reforms was the fact that, despite numerous bloody episodes, many white men gained voting rights and many constitutions were written.

Another significant development of the democratic movements of midcentury was the rise in women's consciousness not only as partners in democratic change but as specific groups who should benefit from those changes. Beginning in the mid-nineteenth century, groups of women and people of color began to measure democracy by the degree to which it incorporated them and their interests. As a result of the 1848 revolution in France and the sudden possibility of slave rebellions in its colonies, the provisional government of France freed the slaves in all of its colonies, including the Caribbean islands of Martinique and Guadeloupe, and Senegal in West Africa. But despite many attempts to end slavery in the United States, the Emancipation Proclamation liberated slaves only in the states that had "risen in rebellion against the United States," and who, after January 1, 1863, would "then, thenceforward, and forever [be] free." Slaves in the rest of the United States did not gain their freedom until the Thirteenth Amendment to the Constitution was ratified at the end of December 1865 proclaiming that the Constitution would allow "Neither slavery nor involuntary servitude, except as punishment for crime whereof the party shall have been duly convicted . . ."[15] One of the main goals of radical Republicans in the United States was to pass constitutional amendments to assure the freedom and civil rights of men liberated from slavery. With most states that had joined the confederacy temporarily excluded from participation in Congress until 1868 and with a number of black senators and representatives voting until 1878, the Fourteenth, and Fifteenth amendments were added to the Constitution, insuring all men rights of citizenship, including due process of the law, and granting formerly enslaved men the right to vote and be elected to office. The Nineteenth Amendment, which made women of all colors citizens with the right to vote, did not take effect until 1920.

Women's struggles for suffrage, like other democratic campaigns, had a long history. In 1840, Elizabeth Cady, an activist in both the temperance and antislavery movements, married Henry Stanton, a member of the American and Foreign Anti-Slavery Society, and accompanied him to the World's Anti-Slavery Convention in London. Hoping to take part, she and Lucretia Mott, an official delegate of two antislavery societies in Pennsylvania, and five other women delegates from the United States were refused seating because of their gender. For many Quakers like Lucretia Mott, being a Quaker entailed belief in human equality and, although Elizabeth Cady Stanton had grown up in a privileged household, she too had suffered worse losses than being excluded from a conference. But the rejection entailed more than a mere slight. As young as Stanton was, she had spent hour after hour in her eminent father's law office along with his law clerks, and knew that justice consisted in rights. Slaves needed to be free and so did women. The slight was equally memorable for Mott, a Quaker minister who said that the issue of women's rights "was the most important question of my life from an early age." Mott, though twenty years older and far more religious, inspired her young colleague. Stanton claims to have thought that "When [she] first heard from [Mott's] lips that [I] had the same right to think for myself that Luther, Calvin and John Knox had, and the same right to be guided by my convictions . . . I felt a new born sense of dignity and freedom."[16]

For eight years after their initial meeting in London, Elizabeth Cady Stanton and Lucretia Mott continued their political activism in different moral reform movements, and raised their families, living far apart from one another and communicating only occasionally. But in July 1848, Stanton and Mott were invited to the home of a mutual friend and instantly resumed their conversation about women's rights. In a moment of inspiration and rage that may have seemed like a calling, the two women and three friends, including Mott's sister, decided to organize a conference to meet the following week. Since Mott was a renowned speaker in the abolitionist movement, they put an ad in the local paper announcing her appearance.

Unsure at first about how to proceed, one of the organizers rummaging through various papers came upon the Declaration of Independence, and the four women began playing around with the language.[17] In three or four days, Stanton sat down and wrote the "Declaration of Sentiments," which was read aloud to the audience of people who lived nearby in Seneca Falls and Rochester, New York. Nearly 300 people including about thirty men filled the audience on the first day of the two-day conference. Substituting "men and women" everywhere that the Declaration of Independence had put "men," the revised document explained that, "We hold these truths to be self-evident: that all men and women are created equal . . ." and went on from there, listing the way the law discriminated against women as workers and wives who lacked control over their own wages and other property. Barred from any institution of higher education, women could not aspire to professional careers. If their husbands betrayed them, they had no rights to complain to the law. And if he divorced them, they lost their children. Stanton's solution? Demand women's rights to vote. Although her collaborators thought she would undermine all their support if she made such a radical demand, she insisted. And with the help of the editor of the *North Star*, the famous abolitionist, former slave, and journalist

Frederick Douglass, the convention narrowly supported the demand for suffrage.[18]

Despite the fact that Seneca Falls was a small town, newspapers all over the East coast responded. The Associated Press, first organized the previous May 1848 as a consortium of six of New York City's most powerful newspapers, carried news about the conference at Seneca Falls and another women's rights convention that Elizabeth Cady Stanton and Lucretia Mott addressed in nearby Rochester a few weeks later. Most of the papers ridiculed the idea of women's rights, arguing that being a wife was a higher calling. Others said the demand for political and social rights would make women laughing stocks. But aside from the humor, *The New York Herald* published the whole "Declaration," and Horace Greeley, the editor of the *New York Tribune*, went against his personal distaste for women's political aspirations, and admitted that "however unwise and mistaken the demand, it is but the assertion of a natural right and as such must be conceded."[19]

In September, 1848, Stanton responded to some of her critics. Addressing an article that appeared in the *National Reformer* of Rochester: "one might suppose from the articles that you find in some papers, that there were editors so ignorant as to believe that the chief object of these Conventions was to seat every lord at the head of a cradle, and to clothe every woman in her lord's attire." Ridiculing the persistent fear of role reversals, she explained that, "the real object[s] of our recent Conventions at Rochester and Seneca Falls . . . was simply our own inalienable rights, our duties, our true sphere. If God has assigned a sphere to man and woman, we claim the right to judge ourselves of His design in reference to us, and we accord to [every] man the same privilege. We think a man has quite enough in his life to find out his own individual calling, without being taxed to decide where every woman belongs."[20] In the long years that followed, Stanton used the press as one of the main weapons she and the suffrage movement employed to secure the vote.

Like the women's suffrage movement in the United States that owed so much to its religious origins among Quakers, Methodists, and Congregationalist Protestants, a far-reaching Christian peasant revolution with some democratic overtones emerged in China in 1848. Of southern China's eighteen provinces, sixteen joined a revolution between 1848 and 1865. The movement called the Taiping Rebellion attempted to overthrow the Qing or Manchu Dynasty that had ruled China since the middle of the seventeenth century. The British defeat of China in the first Opium War (1839–42) in which the Chinese government had tried to resist the forced sale of opium that turned millions of ordinary Chinese into hopeless drug addicts, confirmed the inability of the Chinese authorities to control their own ports, especially those around Canton. Conditions grew worse, but the Taiping Rebellion, which swept China and led to between twenty- and thirty-million deaths in one of the most destructive wars of modern times, led to some unintended democratic consequences, including increased opportunities for decision-making by both male and female peasants.

The revolution led by Hong Xiuquan, an ethnic Hakka and Christian convert, envisioned an entirely new social system in which large numbers of illiterate men and women could democratically participate. The Hakka people had migrated south during the Middle Ages, and in the nineteenth century they largely consisted of humble miners, boat people, charcoal burners, masons, barbers, blacksmiths, and tenant farmers, many organized into separate secret societies.[21] Hakka women enjoyed far more freedom than the majority Han group, and Hakka women were drawn to the new movement.

"Taiping" roughly means peace or equal justice and it was the ultimate goal of the rebellion that Hong Xiuquan launched. His ideology found institutional expression in the secret mutual aid groups that protected themselves against intense government surveillance on one hand and banditry on the other.[22] Around 1836, Hong Xiuquan suffered a nervous breakdown when he became one of many applicants who failed the civil service exams three times and thus lost the ability to become a scholar or state official. Following his collapse, he underwent a religious conversion after reading a Christian tract that urged readers to seek Jesus Christ and to observe the Ten Commandments. After a brief period of study with an American Southern Baptist missionary, Hong went off on his own, had fevered visions, and became convinced that he was Christ's younger brother. Losing his job as a village school teacher in 1844 as a result of his beliefs, he and his convert cousin set off as traveling preachers.[23]

Hong and the group that came to be known as the God Worshippers Society found many adherents among the Hakka minority and mobilized women as well as men into the armies they formed to promote their religious and cultural practices. The Taiping leaders called for female education, access to land, and rights to take democratized exams to enter the bureaucracy, though they did not call for a constitutional government. In their efforts to enable Chinese peasants to achieve their place as functioning citizens, they wanted to outlaw polygamy and prostitution along with female foot-binding. In the community, Believers were forbidden from smoking opium, drinking alcohol, or holding slaves, though some leaders ignored these rules and even created harems.[24]

The democratic character of the Taiping benefitted from what anthropologists call "laterally bonded ties" of brothers and sisters, rather than of hierarchically structured units that subordinated women and children to father figures. In hopes of establishing a community based on universal brother- and sisterhood free to share all their belongings and govern themselves at least locally, a diverse group of southern Chinese people set out to create a social utopia.[25]

In March 1853, the Taiping took the great city of Nanjing, which they renamed the Heavenly Capital. There they attempted to establish a community of people who enjoyed all goods equally. An American missionary who visited them in May 1854 reported that the population seemed well-fed, well-clothed, and quite content, and that they seemed to govern themselves through local committees. The drive to equality institutionalized in local organizations contributed to demands that anyone found advancing at the expense of others would be severely punished.

As the Taiping grew to become a force of more than a million highly disciplined troops who were supposed to protect the common people from abuse, they divided land according to age and sex in order to assure everyone food, while surpluses were stored for the general good. Although Taiping leaders censored books, the variety and volume of publications—including new school texts, classical literature, and history—permitted a certain degree of independent thought among the small part of the population that was literate. Had some system of local government developed and prospered, the Taiping might have been able to maintain itself over a long period.

As it was, Hong Jen-kan (Hong Rengan) was able to replace his cousin Hong Xiuquan, who was increasingly suffering mental delusions. Under Hong Jen-kan and his advisors, voting took place sporadically, and intellectual life flourished in the larger towns, where public debates often took place.[26] Hong Jen-kan and his aides permitted publications similar to newspapers in all the major cities of southern China, supplementing them with the widespread suggestion boxes in which ordinary people could make their will known. The degree to which any of these mechanisms worked in a society in which most people were illiterate remains questionable. But the attempt Hong Jen-kan and his compatriots made to open up conversations between the rulers and the governed went to the heart of one of the weaknesses in every known democratic system until the advent of social media, namely the lack of mechanisms for exchanging ideas between the masses and their leaders.[27] While it is not clear how often the ideas from the suggestion boxes and news bureaus ever reached the Taiping decision-makers, the mere act of being able to think that they might, constituted a major advance in democratic initiatives.

Many historians have dismissed the Taiping as religious fanatics, especially in their opposition to landowners and practitioners of Confucianism. Others view them as proponents of some form of democracy in their wish to substitute the rule of law for the rule of religious revelation and in their egalitarian division of agricultural resources. By 1863, however, whatever relatively democratic local practices existed floundered as the Taiping leaders engaged in internecine struggles and the army of Great Britain joined with the Qing forces of Northern China to defeat the Taiping, slaughtering their leaders in the process.[28] Yet hundreds of thousands of Taiping peasants went on fighting until August 1871 to maintain their modicum of self-government and their local control of land while others fled to Hong Kong and even the United States in search of work and freedom from persecution.

The suffrage movements in Australia, New Zealand, and Finland were the first to win women the vote. Australian feminists like Louisa Lawson believed that in such a large country as hers women needed voting rights in order to ensure that their voices be heard. "A woman's opinions are useless to her, she may suffer unjustly, she may be wronged, but she has no power to weightily petition against man's laws, no representatives to urge her views, her only method to produce release, redress, or change, is to ceaselessly agitate."[29]

One important act of agitation among men as well as women was the effort to end slavery and create a multiracial society in Cuba. And few Cubans gave more to this effort than Antonio Maceo. One of nine children of Marcos Maceo and Mariana Grajales Coello, two free black immigrants to Cuba, Antonio Maceo grew up near the city of Santiago where he and his family marketed and sold food products that they grew on their small farms. Like many of their neighbors, the Maceos maintained an uneasy alliance with the western white merchants and the refinery and plantation owners around Havana. When war between Spain and Cuba broke out in 1868, Antonio and his brother José, who were both in their early twenties, immediately joined up and Antonio soon caught the attention of general Máximo Gómez, one of the leaders of the Eastern forces.

Antonio Maceo, one of the leading early practitioners of guerrilla warfare, fought for Cuba's independence from Spain from 1868 to 1878, throughout 1879, and then from 1895 until his death in 1896. In March 1878, when his allies agreed to a truce without demanding the complete abolition of slavery, he responded that "a man who is fighting for a principle and has a high regard for his honor and reputation can[not] sell himself while there is still at least a chance of saving his principles by dying. . . . Men like me fight only in the cause of liberty and will smash their guns rather than submit." The Granger Collection, New York

The immediate cause of the war was the 1868 toppling of the Queen of Spain and the decision of one portion of the white slave-holding sugar growers and refiners to fight for their independence. As early as 1867, planters and owners of sugar refineries in Cuba's eastern or *Oriente* area had been meeting to consider how to gain greater rights. In October 1868, one month after the queen was overthrown, one of those involved in those meetings, Carlos Manuel de Céspedes, a slave-holding owner of a sugar plantation, rose up against Spain, freed his slaves, and invited them as citizens to join the fight for Cuban independence. Céspedes's main supporters came from eastern Cuba where there was a large contingent of free Afro-Cuban farmers who grew tobacco and food crops, as the Maceo family did. In the western part of the island, Havana's merchants and sugar plantation and refinery owners were divided over what to do. Many wanted the Spanish to leave, but most of the Western planters either hoped to hold on to their ties with Spain or wanted to hold on to their slaves and were unwilling to collaborate with free black and mulatto farmers. Above all, whether royalist or republican, the wealthy western slave-owning planters, merchants, and refiners for whom sugar was white gold did not want the war to be fought on their territory. And without the invasion of the west, it would be impossible to drive out the Spanish forces.

Maceo quickly rose through the ranks of the forces in the eastern part of Cuba where most of the Ten Years' War (1868–78) was waged. Perhaps his early familiarity with the back roads of the mountainous eastern Cuba or his ties to other small farmers and storekeepers amply suited him to make and maintain the alliances that waging guerrilla war required. Without ready arms supplies, the eastern army fought with machetes as well as rifles and depended on maintaining and having his troops maintain friendly relations with the farmers from whom they got their supplies. Whatever the difficulties, Maceo became a hero to some and a dangerous threat to others because of his success in resisting the Spanish troops.

Maceo and his troops' effectiveness also suffered from the racism of some of his supposed allies. In 1876, after eight years of fighting against Spain, Maceo wrote to the President of the Cuban revolutionary government, claiming that he had heard from various groups in various settings "that a small circle exists which has manifested to the Government that it 'did not wish to serve under my orders because I belong to the colored race.' And later, through different channels, I have learned that they are now accusing me of 'showing favoritism to the colored over the white officers in my command' . . . [B]y this method they hope to destroy me as they have not been able to do so by other means. They are trying to do this to a man who entered the revolution for no other reason than to shed his blood to see the slaves and his country free . . . I must protest energetically and with all my strength that neither now nor at any other time am I to be regarded as an advocate of a Negro Republic or anything of that sort."[30]

The War became stalemated and the Cubans and Spanish authorities agreed to a treaty. But Maceo and his brother José Maceo refused to sign the accords ending the Ten Years' War, in which their father and 250,000 other Cubans had fought and died. Antonio Maceo explained why he viewed the treaty as a betrayal: "Our policy is to free the slaves, because the era of the whip and of Spanish cynicism has come to an end, and we ought to form a new Republic assimilated with our sisters Santo Domingo and Haiti."[31] Although richer Cubans and resident Spanish men gained the right to elect representatives to the Spanish parliament, poor whites and Afro-Cubans still lacked political representation. To make matters more complicated, the Spanish repeatedly played on white Cuban fears of early nineteenth-century slave uprisings in Haiti and in Jamaica in order to provoke racism against Maceo and other black Cuban leaders, and thereby undermine efforts towards democratization and independence. Maceo's reference to uniting in some way with Santo Domingo and Haiti would have thrown terror into the hearts of many white planters and merchants.

After the Ten Years' War, Maceo, his brother, and a small number of patriots from eastern Cuba fought on for another year. Unable to rebuild their forces, Maceo then traveled to Santo Domingo, Honduras, and finally Costa Rica, keeping in touch with others eager to go back to Cuba to drive out the Spaniards. Entering Cuba somewhat clandestinely in 1890, he received a warm welcome before being driven out by the government. He then joined José Martí's Cuban Revolutionary Party at its founding in 1892 and returned to fight in Cuba in February 1895. After a year and a half, he died in battle on December 7, 1896.

Cuban intellectual, poet, and leader of the independence movement José Martí understood the delicate balance necessary to achieving a united front against the Spanish and counteracted Spanish strategies to divide Cubans according to race by emphasizing the importance of freedom for Cubans of all races in the independence movement and by highlighting already existing fraternity among all groups.. Ricardo Batrell, an Afro-Cuban who joined the independence movement at age fifteen, while still illiterate, went on to write the only known memoir by a Black soldier of the war of 1895. In it he recalls a story of reciprocal aid between a white colonel and his black assistant, both badly wounded in a battle, but who together helped each other survive. He concludes, "Isn't it true, reader, that it would hearten us immensely to believe that humanity had been perfected . . .? Yes, we may believe it, because that was democracy, with all its beautiful attributes. Because [at that moment] there existed 'reciprocity'—a reciprocity that all civilized peoples, nations, and men struggle to attain."[32] Many multiracial countries still strive for that reciprocity.

CHAPTER 5

Social Revolution and Participatory Democracy

Emiliano Zapata, a mixed-race or *mestizo* farmer and horse trainer from Anenecuilco, a village in the province of Morelos, about fifty miles from Mexico City, helped shape the Mexican Revolution of 1910 to 1920. For about a century the villagers of Anenecuilco had been fighting against the owners of a ranch called "Hospital" to regain control over village land, water, and pasture rights. When reformers like Francisco Madero, intent on overthrowing the dictator Porfirio Díaz, who had ruled Mexico since 1876, launched a campaign in 1910 under the slogan of "Effective Suffrage and No Reelection," Zapata and his neighbors joined Madero. But they wanted more than elections. They wanted "Land and Freedom" (*Tierra y Libertad*) by which they meant control over land that had been expropriated from them and freedom to make decisions about how to manage their lives.

Porfirio Díaz, a rich businessman, had become president of Mexico in 1876 just as Mexico became increasingly attractive to European and North American investors, and he went on to hold six subsequent terms. As corruption deepened, legislators and journalists who opposed the sale of the country's resources to rich foreigners landed in prison. Usurping power by refusing to hold elections, Díaz and his cronies sold many of the forests and communal lands to foreign and local entrepreneurs who established lumbering, turpentine, fruit, cotton, and sugar plantations, frequently enslaving indigenous people, reducing mixed-race or *mestizo* workers to debt slavery, and exploiting and sexually abusing poor women of all races. Seventeen percent of the workforce of foreign and locally owned textile factories was made up of women, who earned exceedingly low wages and lacked any form of protection on the job.[1] In many places in Mexico, peasants who needed food or clothing that they could have produced themselves were forced to buy it at inflated prices from the company store, while serving as

Emiliano Zapata, portrayed in a mural at the Mexican Ministry of Education, wears the large white hat common to southern Mexican peasants and holds a sign calling for "Tierra y Libertad" (Land and Freedom). His image has survived ouside Mexico as well as inside because he promoted the collective interests of small farmers whose land had been taken from them and because he lived out his creed: "I want to die a slave to principles, not to men." Secretaria de Educación Publica, Mexico City D.F., Mexico Schalkwijk / Art Resource, NY © 2014 Banco de México Diego Rivera Frida Kahlo Museums Trust, Mexico, D.F. / Artists Rights Society (ARS), New York

cultivators and harvesters on plantations that they themselves had previously administered collectively through relatively democratic village councils. Failure to produce quotas of lumber or fruit led to deductions from laborers' annual wages. Frequently, at the end of the year, the worker could not pay his or her debt, could not leave, and had to stay on until he or she had paid it, which almost never happened.

More favorable agricultural tenancy agreements disappeared, and the common lands were sold to investors who wanted to consolidate their control, thus throwing even small landowning farmers like Zapata's family and neighbors into disarray. Although the Zapata family managed to keep their land, many Mexican peasants became tenants, sharecroppers, or simply landless day laborers on land they had previously owned collectively. Periodic efforts to retrieve common land and water rights, gain suffrage, and help reshape their societies into democratic institutions had ended in failure.

Local councils in Europe and Latin America had often allocated tasks and adjudicated disputes over common resources. But once the land was privatized, local peasant councils could no longer exercise power over land on which they had lived for generations. By 1909, twenty-eight private landowners controlled 77 percent of the land around Anenecuilco and equal or greater amounts elsewhere. The large estates such as Hospital privatized more and more of the common land once used as free as pasture for their herds.[2]

At thirty, Zapata was a well-respected community leader. Between 1902 and 1905, he worked with neighboring farmers to regain their land, and in 1904 he joined them on a trip to the National Archives in search of written documents that they believed would prove their previous collective ownership of local land, water, and pastures. Like farmers from Puebla, Oaxaca, and other areas around Mexico City, Zapata and his neighbors continued to work for political reform while trying to recapture the land they believed was theirs. For example, they actively participated in the gubernatorial elections of 1908, and were disillusioned when the disputed election of February 1909 once again handed power to Díaz's candidates. In an effort to solve local problems that directly affected their daily lives, Zapata joined his neighbors when they seized some of the lands that they regarded as theirs. For instance, on April 25, 1909, he pitched in when they decided to plant crops on disputed property. His willingness to join in the effort further established him as a peasant leader who could be trusted.[3]

Francisco Madero, a businessman and large landowner in the northern state of Coahuila, who in 1909 began a campaign to oust Díaz through electoral reform, called on Zapata and other local leaders to join him. Madero's successful campaign to win the presidency in 1910 led Díaz to have him imprisoned, from where he called for a revolution to overthrow the regime. The Mexican Revolution began in 1910, and led to ten years of civil war in which different generals and various local leaders dominated different regions of the country while fighting to gain control of Mexico City. Zapata initially joined the revolution on Madero's side, but when he realized that Madero had no intention of returning the land to the peasants, he and his supporters attempted to formulate their own democratic program. As a result of the fighting, Díaz was forced to flee the country in 1911, and Madero was assassinated that same year.

During the war, which ended in 1920, Zapata attempted to carry out a revolution within the revolution in Morelos until he too was assassinated in 1919. One of Zapata's chief advisors was Dolores Jiménez y Muro. Born in 1848, she fought for educational reforms and improved working conditions for factory workers. Committed to democratization of every aspect of social life, she also fought for improved housing and reduced rental costs.[4] But, most of all, she tried to help Zapata restore village lands to the collective control of local people. Dolores Jiménez y Muro and Zapata's close personal friend, Otilio Montaña, a socialist school teacher, poet, and left-wing journalist, helped write the Zapatista's "Plan de Ayala" that demanded restitution of land and water rights that had been privatized by local landowners. The Plan de Ayala, whose slogan was "Liberty, Justice, and Law," claimed that it was the task of the big estate owners, rather than the peasant claimants, to prove their titles. Furthermore it called for the distribution to the villagers of one-third of all forests, water, and land held in estates.[5] As the war dragged on, General Venustiano Carranza managed to take over Mexico City in 1917. By military force, Carranza became president of Mexico from 1917 to 1920, surprising many of his liberal critics by instituting sweeping reforms with the goal of uniting workers, peasants, and the business community that were all suffering from years of war.

His principal reform, the 1917 Constitution, attempted to institutionalize social rights as part of Mexico's reunification program. The social content of the Constitution was so compelling that some think that both the Soviet Union and the new Weimar Republic in Germany modeled their own constitutions on it in 1918 and 1919, respectively. Article 123 of the Mexican Constitution limited the length of the work day to eight hours—a right that workers in the United States did not gain until the Wagner Act of 1935. Mexico specifically established the right of workers to strike, the right to appeal from being fired, and the right to at least one day's rest every week. It went on to incorporate freedom of assembly, free and compulsory primary education, freedom to publish without censorship, the right to petition, freedom of expression, the right to travel freely, trial by jury, and freedom from expropriation except for public use. Article 27 required that foreigners abide by Mexican law in their use of land, water, petroleum, or other natural resources, all of which belonged to the Mexican state. The communal lands taken under Díaz were to revert to the villages, communities, small farms, and towns from which they had been taken. Workers gained the right to strike though employers could also layoff and even lockout workers when profits dropped. Maternity protection for three months prior to childbirth, paid maternity leave afterward, and the right to nurse one's infant for two half-hour periods during the workday were also included.[6] The Mexican Constitution also made powerful commitments to equal rights "avoiding privileges of race, class, sex, or persons," as Article 3 proclaimed. Yet the Mexican Constitution, despite its many achievements, joined other democratic countries in refusing to grant women the right to vote. This was especially surprising in Mexico where Hermila Galindo, an ardent feminist, served as Carranza's secretary from 1917 to 1920. Although she agitated along with an active Mexican suffragist movement, they could not persuade even progressive legislators to grant women voting privileges, a right they only succeeded in winning in 1947.

The struggle for suffrage varied enormously from country to country. Suffragists in New Zealand were the first to gain the vote and their main adversaries were the national liquor lobby. They led the fight against women's votes in part because the Women's Christian Temperance Union (WCTU) was prominent among its advocates. In 1885, the WCTU, which had been founded in the United States as a social reform movement, spread to New Zealand where it was dedicated to relieving poverty especially among young people, ending violence against women, improving hospital service, and reforming prisons, as well as winning women's suffrage. Using direct action including mobilization, petitioning Parliament, and organizing letter writing campaigns, New Zealand's suffrage movement finally won the vote in 1893.[7]

In Belgium, where the Socialist Labor party in the late nineteenth century first coined the phrase "one man, one vote" to prevent wealthy citizens from voting wherever they held property, the conservatives provocatively asked why not demand "one person, one vote?" Paradoxically many conservatives, liberals, and socialists all over the world shared the view that, despite suffragist activity in each of their respective countries, women would automatically vote for conservatives. Because of that view among others, in countries like Chile, Mexico, and France, most liberal politicians continued to oppose women's suffrage in national elections until after the Second World War. The exclusion of women from full citizenship was a major indication of the fact that even in countries fiercely committed to democracy patriarchal attitudes perpetuated the exclusion of women from the rights and duties of full citizenship.

Democratic movements seeking to create representative institutions repeatedly appeared in the twentieth century. In St. Petersburg, Russia, the traditional center of Russian government and the city with the most international connections, intellectuals and workers had long organized themselves into political clubs and clandestine trade unions. In 1905, following the massacre known as Bloody Sunday, during which 100 to 300 people were killed demanding an end to war with Japan and the creation of a democratic legislature, committees of all stripes gathered to consider what was to be done. Hoping to assuage opposition without actually relinquishing power, the tsar and his advisors established a Duma or parliament with such highly restrictive rules that workers, soldiers, and sailors were almost completely excluded from voting. As the metallurgical workers began to strike, they proclaimed their political intentions, calling for what they called a political strike. Their goal was to summon "a Constituent Assembly on the basis of universal, equal, direct, and secret suffrage to introduce a democratic republic in Russia."[8] Peasant farmers, unable to pay their rents or win a hearing from the landowners, began to destroy their property. On October 13, the workers of St. Petersburg formed their own representative organization, councils known as *soviets*, in which there would be one representative for every 500 workers. A few days later, as demands for equity overtook the country, the tsarist ministers seemingly decided that they were not powerful enough to repress all the opposing forces. Instead, they extended the powers of the Duma, making it into a moderate legislative assembly with various layers of power. Although the lower-middle class and workers would have representation only in the final stages of its deliberations, the decision to extend the franchise rather than simply repress all opponents seemed to bode well for future democratic rule.

Failure to recognize its own military weakness or to recall what fighting on one's own soil meant drew Russians as well as other leading European, Asian, and Middle Eastern nations and their colonies into the First World War in 1914. Socialists such as the Polish-born Rosa Luxemburg might excoriate her fellow legislators in the German parliament or Reichstag as hypocrites for voting war credits permitting their country to enter the First World War, but many patriots of all classes viewed the coming war as an opportunity to gain their fortunes and expand the territory their nation controlled. In most democratic countries, the decision to go to war, in the final analysis, won the enthusiastic support of the majority of elected officials.

More than any of the adversaries in the First World War, the Russian imperial army faced devastating losses since they were the sole defenders of the Eastern Front against the Austro-Hungarian, German,

Rosa Luxemburg (back row, center), one of the foremost early twentieth century Marxist intellectuals, took part in the sixth International Socialist Congress in Amsterdam in August 1904 along with other leading socialist theorists, Karl Kautsky and Victor Adler. In a pamphlet she published during the First World War, she argued that it was "foolish and mad to imagine that we need only survive the war, like a rabbit waiting out the storm under a bush, in order to fall happily back into the old routine once it is over. The world war has altered the conditions of our struggle and, most of all, it has changed us." Visual Documents, International Institute of Social History (Amsterdam)

and Turkish military forces. As the bloodbath ensued, different groups of pacifists, nationalists, socialists, and democrats on all sides of the struggle attempted to end the bloodshed. In exile in Switzerland, Vladimir I. Lenin was one among many Russians who believed that his country would be destroyed if the fighting continued.

In the era leading up to the First World War, certain female pacifists tried to extend notions of democracy to include previously underrepresented demands. Rosika Schwimmer, the daughter of a wealthy Hungarian biologist and his wife, grew up in Budapest. When her father went bankrupt at the end of the nineteenth century, she took a job as a bookkeeper. Alert to power relations and sensitive to those unable to win rights to govern themselves, she joined and soon became the president of the National Association of Women Office Workers and

Rosika Schwimmer, feminist, pacifist, and litigant for citizenship before the
Supreme Court of the United States, constantly tested democratic procedures.
When she was denied citizenship in 1926 for refusing to pledge to serve in the
armed forces, which at the time neither recruited women nor allowed people
her age to serve, she took her case to the Supreme Court. In a minority opinion
(United States v. Schwimmer, 1929), Justice Oliver Wendell Holmes argued that
"if there is any principle of the Constitution that more imperatively calls for
attachment than any other it is the principle of free thought—not free thought
for those who agree with us but freedom for the thought that we hate." Library
of Congress LC-DIG-ggbain-18633

helped form the Hungarian Association of Working Women. Like others focused on winning rights to participate in governing their societies, she joined international organizations. Beginning with the International Women's Suffrage Alliance (IWSA) made up of women's suffrage organizations from ten countries, she contacted feminists, peace activists, and world leaders, increasingly convinced that no democratic reforms were possible unless war was resisted and then abolished.

By 1909, Schwimmer had relocated to London where she served as IWSA's press secretary. Joining forces with a leading Dutch feminist Aletta Jacobs and American feminist and Hull House Settlement founder Jane Addams, Schwimmer helped organize the International [Peace] Congress of Women in 1915 at the Hague, where participants called for an end to the war and equal rights for women. As Jacobs explained optimistically "Women will soon have political power. Woman suffrage and permanent peace will go together. When a country is in a state of mind to grant the vote to its women, it is a sign that that country is ripe for permanent peace."[9] Schwimmer's associates who sometimes violated national laws to sue for peace often faced imprisonment for their pacifism. But they and other activists formed what was later called the Women's International League for Peace and Freedom and continued to struggle for peace.

As casualties mounted during the First World War and production failed to keep pace with demand, many in Russia tired of war and began to search for ways to end their country's participation. Of the 7.5 million Russian men drafted, half of the two million Russians who ultimately died or disappeared had done so by early 1917. The government was weak and groups on all sides were considering what to do. Food prices, particularly the price per pound of rye bread, the staple of working class diets in Petrograd, rose from three kopeks in 1913 to eighteen kopeks in 1916. Even soap, necessary to maintaining clean clothes and human dignity, rose 245 percent in 1917 Petrograd. With most able-bodied men in the armed forces, women made up 43 percent of all factory workers. Whether married or merely members of large families, women worked sixteen-hour days in the factories or sweatshops and then had to wait in line for bread. Often, the bread, the major item of consumption in working-class families, ran out by the time a woman got to the front of the line.

In February 1917, the groups trying to end the war urged the women of St. Petersburg (renamed Petrograd during the war) not to celebrate International Woman's Day (February 23 on the Julian calendar, observed in Russia, but March 8 in the West) since the city was a powder keg. Against their wishes, poor women—who, along with their richer sisters, lacked the vote—engaged in direct action. They marched over the bridges from the working-class districts to the center of the city, where male and female factory workers joined them. They went to the bread lines and, gathering crowds, marched to the wealthy neighborhoods where the nobility, merchants, and government officials lived. They marched to the Duma and then to the tsar's Winter Palace, repeatedly calling for "Bread and Peace" and an end to the war. On February 25, two days after the insurrection began, the tsar ordered the military to act. The general in charge later remembered his confusion "How to 'stop'? When they asked for bread, we gave them bread and that was the end of it. But when the flags are inscribed 'down with the autocracy' it's no longer a question of bread. But what then? The tsar had ordered—we had to shoot."[10] But, when the cavalry disobeyed orders and refused to attack the women, the government fell and its collapse launched what became known as the February Revolution.

The first phase of the revolution had succeeded in intensifying the possibilities for moderate democratic reform in Russia, but the independent *soviets*, or democratic councils that along with the parliament had emerged in 1905, refused to recognize the authority of the provisional government after July 1917. Many of the parties on the left believed that neither peace nor political stability would follow until Russia withdrew from the War. In October 1917, the Bolsheviks or Communists, along with a wide array of people dissatisfied with the progress the Duma was making to end the war, carried out a more sweeping revolution.

When the soldiers and sailors, organized into self-governing, democratic *soviets*, stormed the tsar's Winter Palace on October 25, 1917, the Russian empire collapsed. Those who carried out this maneuver had long debated their own conditions and the possibilities for a more equitable and democratic political system. As they passed quickly from their icy barracks, they overran the tsar's palace and arrested the tsar, his whole family, and the commander-in-chief of the armed forces. At the same time, Lenin entered into negotiations with the German high command to withdraw Russia from the First World War.

The revolution generated a counter-revolution, as most twentieth-century revolutions did. With the defenders of the tsar and many liberals, leftists, and regional nationalists periodically against them, the Bolsheviks increasingly consolidated their power in fewer and fewer hands. Whether or not individual Bolsheviks believed in democracy, fewer and fewer of them attempted to defend it. Lenin, in fact, opposed democracy *per se*, viewing it as the rule of the bourgeoisie. But other radicals and revolutionaries embraced it as the only possible governmental system that would enable ordinary people to use the skills they had to gain the higher good.

The Polish independent communist Rosa Luxemburg watched the Russian Revolution unfold from a German jail cell. She had been arrested for her participation in an attempt to carry out a communist revolution in 1918 following Germany's defeat in the First World War. Shortly before she died at the hands of a right-wing gang in January 1919, she composed a letter, outlining her view of the Bolsheviks at the end of a little more than their first year of rule. She wrote that "without general elections, without unrestricted freedom of the press and the assembly, without a free struggle of opinion, life dies out in every public institution, becomes a mere semblance of life, in which only the bureaucracy remains as the active element. Public life gradually falls asleep, a few experience direct rule. Among them, in reality only a dozen outstanding heads do the leading and an elite of the working class is invited from time to time to meetings where they are to applaud the speeches of the leaders, and to approve proposed resolutions unanimously—at bottom, then, a clique affair—a dictatorship, to be sure, not the dictatorship of the proletariat, however, but only the dictatorship in the bourgeois sense. . . . Yes, we can go even further. . . . Such conditions must inevitably cause a brutalization of public life. . . ."[11] An uprising in February and March 1921 of soviets made up of soldiers, sailors, and workers at the Kronstadt military base near St. Petersburg was brutally repressed, thus ending until 1989 any concentrated efforts to create popular democratic institutions in Russia.

If Lenin, Leon Trotsky, and the other Bolsheviks, social revolutionaries, and anarchists did not understand what would transpire if they repressed the very people who had brought them to power in hope of participating in a democratic society, they had learned nothing from the democratic revolutions that preceded them. The turning point for every revolution facing fervid criticism or a counter-revolution is how far the democratic government is willing to adopt autocratic policies simply to retain power. Almost every twentieth-century revolution, including those that attempted to promote democratic practices, responded to attack by centralizing authority and ultimately creating new, authoritarian structures. But that need not always be the case.

In fact, democratic attempts to resist unjust authority continued to be plentiful as people used old institutions and created new ones to gain more control over the well-being of their communities. Women in British-ruled Southeastern Nigeria, for instance, mobilized to resist taxes that threatened to impoverish them at the beginning of the Great Depression. In 1861, claiming to help end the slave trade in western Africa, the British had annexed the port of Lagos, and in 1912 they added other colonies in northern and southern portions of the territory to form the Colony and Protectorate of Nigeria. While maintaining control over defense and public works, the British imposed a new class of judges and tax collectors called warrant chiefs to govern local areas of Nigeria. Although warrant chiefs had traditionally ruled the northern areas of the country, southern Nigeria had consisted of a series of monarchies and republics, ruled by committees of older men. During the precolonial and early colonial periods, local women had decentralized governments that included mothers' councils that ruled as popular courts in disputes among women, between husbands and wives, and between men and women. Older women had also formed committees to regulate relations between the sexes and control the local trade in palm oil and palm kernels used to manufacture soap. The introduction of an entirely different political system of warrant chiefs, generally young men loyal to the British rather than to local officials, the imposition of new taxes, and the draft of male laborers to build roads and lay railroad tracks, caused local people in southeastern Nigeria to resist British authorities.[12]

As the production of palm products collapsed in 1929 as a result of the drought that accompanied the Great Depression, local women, who were economically autonomous from local men and had gender-based political and economic organizations, faced new government censuses. Since men were forced to pay property taxes in 1927 shortly after submitting to a census of their goods and property, women feared a similar fate. As the census began in late November 1929, women from a variety of villages and ethnic groups in Owerri and Calabar provinces with a population of more than two-million people, mobilized through their local councils and market networks to challenge the chiefs whom they regarded as unrepresentative and illegitimate. The women met together and attempted to register their complaints with local warrant chiefs, who generally scorned the women's demands. Using networks the women ordinarily employed to summon one another across villages in times of trouble, women from all over the territory marched on the capital city of Aba, demanding exemption from the census and the removal of the chiefs.

The women failed to get the British authorities to hear their petitions, and instead the British called out the troops to suppress the massive women's demonstrations in December 1929. In town after town, the British showed their contempt by riding bikes and cars into the demonstrations, killing and maiming women. In one city, authorities ordered the women to disperse, and when the women refused to follow orders, the troops mowed down thirty women. In Aba in December 1929, the troops panicked and massacred eighteen women, and wounded another eighteen. During the course of the struggle, women poured into the capital and burned the courts and Barclay's Bank in what the British called the Aba Riots and local people referred to as the Women's War.[13]

In early 1930, recognizing the women's demands for more democratic participation in decision-making and accepting the women's temporary rights to refuse taxation, the British rescinded the census, called in government employees and anthropologists to assess the situation, and modified the system. But their reforms ended up lessening the power of women's councils and prohibiting the women from demonstrating.

Elsewhere in the world, eruptions of nationalism and imperialism led certain villagers and their leaders to fight against their own authoritarian governments in order to create democratic systems of power. In China, for example, a group of democratic reformers led by Sun Yat-sen succeeded in overthrowing the Qing Dynasty in 1912 and established the Republic of China. Yat-sen helped form the Nationalist Guomintang (formerly called the Kuomintang) party to carry out democratic reforms. Yet despite the creation of a parliament in 1913 and the growing importance of local magistrates, regional legislatures, and provincial governors, local government failed to prosper, and power continued to reside with local warlords. Although Chinese women participated in creating the new government, they never gained the vote under the Republic. Students who were pessimistic about the commitment of Chinese republicans to the massive social and political changes China required joined Mao Zedong and others to form the Chinese Communist Party in 1919.

At the same time, the Treaty of Versailles that ended the First World War set about reassigning German territory to other powers. Although China expected to regain sovereignty over Shandong (formerly known as Shantung), which the Germans had held as a territorial enclave, the Treaty granted its control to the Japanese, who had aided the French and British during the war. In reaction, on May 4, 1919, university students in Beijing gathered at the Gate of Heavenly Peace in Tiananmen Square to protest the evisceration of China. The students demanded the restoration of Chinese territory and the removal of foreign officials and their troops. Arrests followed the students' march on the home of the Minister of Communication and news of their detention in Beijing spread to Shanghai and other universities. In support of those arrested, other students formed a National Student Union. Opposition spread to workers and merchants and resulted in a widespread boycott of all Japanese products.

In 1919, Chinese students also proclaimed the need for a more democratic government with power lodged in a president and legislature elected by a wide range of citizens. The right-wing Chinese authorities who had taken over the government mowed down the students, beating, raping, and even murdering women students. Like attacks on Black American soldiers returning to St. Louis, Chicago, and Tulsa from fighting in the First World War, the attacks on young Chinese women were designed to put them in their place.

With the repression of the May 4th Movement, competing Nationalists and Communists moved their main struggles to the countryside to engage peasant support for their movements. From the spring of 1929 to the fall of 1934, the Communists, who were simultaneously fighting the Nationalists and Japanese forces that had invaded Nanjing in 1931, retreated to Kiangsi (now Jiangxi) province. The Communists formed soviets of soldiers, workers, and peasants, including women. All adults could vote for the 610 delegates (of whom one-quarter were women) to the First National Soviet Congress that met in November 1931. This congress voted to grant rights of free speech, of assembly, of free education, and of freedom of the press for all workers and peasants, and it committed itself to the liberation of women.[14] The Nationalists also made a bid to win women to their side by granting them rights to choose their own marriage partners and divorce them if need be.

The radical changes both Chinese factions undertook to attract women probably resulted less from the wish to make Chinese women full citizens than from the fact that most Chinese men were soldiers engaged in war, leaving women and old men as the main workers throughout the 1930s. In addition to fighting one another, from 1931 on, the Nationalists and Communists fought separately and together to liberate their country from the Japanese. But paradoxically, the Japanese invasion and occupation left the Communist rural communes in Kiangsi relatively free from the Japanese from 1931 to April 1933, while the Nationalists overran the Communists driving the whole settlement to flee west in what was known as The Great March. In the early 1930s, however,, Chinese women, most of whom had been under the tyranny of landlords and warlords (not to mention fathers and husbands), suddenly became full citizens who not only voted on governing the territory, but allocated resources and supervised production.

Some of the distinctive characteristics of the democratic movements that emerge from social revolutions include a belief in participatory democracy that far exceeds the ideological commitments of other democratic governments or their proponents. When social revolutionary programs either include women participants or take women as important subjects of reform, women's gains as women become the measure of democracy. Elsewhere, as in the case of Mexico, focus on redressing peasant grievances and the presumption that peasants are always gendered male precluded real advances for women qua women. The social movement of Russian women, especially their role in going beyond the desires of the Russian liberal and leftist parties in helping launch the February 1917 Revolution, also contributed to creating some of the possibilities for democracy in Russia. However, despite the introduction of a women's bureau and efforts to engage women workers and peasants in production, neither the leaders of *soviets* nor the more centralized states that crushed them ever really integrated women into the ruling groups. In the case of both Chinese Nationalists and Communists fighting against each other and against the Japanese invaders, Chinese women, even the most disparaged peasants among them, had to be recognized as potential citizens whose participation in government provided the only option for orderly government during the wars that swept China in the 1930s and 1940s.

CHAPTER 6

Civil Disobedience and Racial Justice

The fact that the Second World War was a *world war*, fought by the Allies in the name of "democracy," brought the idea of democracy into question in many places. Often liberation movements in countries that were under the control of the victorious powers assumed that they would gain complete independence from their colonizers. Despite written constitutions, many citizens around the world had been and continued to be denied their civil and political rights, and the situation in India, South Africa, and the American South presented particularly egregious cases at the end of the War. Thus, more than coincidence links the independence movement in India that culminated in India and Pakistan's independence in 1947, the fight to enfranchise all South African citizens that culminated in the 1994 election, and the Montgomery Bus Boycott of 1955–56 that helped engender the Civil Rights Acts of 1964 and 1965 in the United States.

A wave of democratic movements followed the end of the Second World War. Using practices of passive resistance that Mahatma Gandhi first developed between 1906 and 1913 as a young immigrant Indian lawyer in South Africa, masses of people in India, the southern United States, and South Africa confronted powerful governments that discriminated against them. In each instance, people used passive resistance such as boycotts as strategies to shame governments that claimed to be democratic. Racial discrimination in South Africa and the United States depended on a mixture of laws and local practices enforced by violence. When authorities, businessmen, landowners, and mine owners could not get what they wanted by threats, they created laws that undermined the democracies they claimed to uphold.

Africans and Europeans first made contact in South Africa in 1652 at the Cape of Good Hope, near contemporary Cape Town. Although the merchants of the Dutch East India Trading Company and the British merchants who followed them frequently embraced the kind of liberal reforms that John Lilburne and others promoted during the English Revolution, the trading companies had no interest in extending these rights to those they had conquered. For nearly three hundred years, both the Dutch and the British fought against and then suppressed Africans and later Malays and Indians taken as indentured servants to the colonists' sugar plantations in South Africa. Africans of all races and ethnicities resisted, but the superior arms of the Dutch and the British ultimately defeated them. The British at first limited their settlements to the ports, especially Cape Town, Durban, and Port Elizabeth, while the Dutch set up inland farms on land they conquered from African people. But the discovery of diamonds followed by a massive gold rush in the middle and late nineteenth century drew the British into the mines of Kimberly, the gold fields of the Rand around Johannesburg, the Transvaal, and the Orange Free State, where Dutch settlers had established farms on African land. In addition to fighting against groups such as the Zulus, who managed to maintain their independence until the early twentieth century, the British and the Dutch farmers (known later as the Boers or Afrikaners) fought each other between 1899 and 1902, driving the Boers further inland where they seized even more fertile land and reduced numerous African farmers to landless day laborers.

The British, having emerged victorious in the South African War in 1902, secured the safety of their vast mining and business interests by setting up institutions to regulate the cities. Before 1910, South Africa consisted of four separate countries: The Cape Colony, the Orange Free State, The Transvaal, and the Rand or Witwatersrand, each with separate laws and political institutions. Having gained ascendency by the early twentieth century in all but the Free State, the colonists introduced British-style municipal councils, courts, and parliaments, all of which passed and adjudicated laws made by and for whites. And despite the existence of certain democratic institutions in each region, African men and "coloreds,"the name given to people of Khoi descent or people of mixed Asian and African groups, were barred from moving freely from one place to another without internal passports known as "passes."

The language of passes varied, but generally they stipulated how long and under what conditions a worker had to perform certain services, how long he had worked for a specific employer, and under what conditions he had departed. Being fired or simply deciding to work elsewhere might alert future employers to the fact that the worker was likely to stand up for his rights. Without the passes, however, male laborers could not gain other employment or get lodgings. Whenever possible, workers of all races, ethnicities, and sexes resisted the imposition of passes and were moderately successful in Port Elizabeth and East London in the Eastern Cape. The passes were generally designed to secure a steady supply of male labor, but some black and colored men and women fought successfully from 1910 to the late 1950s to end the Pass laws that segregated and controlled the movement of black and colored workers.

Some of the foremost early struggles for democracy in South Africa took place around the demand for equal protection of the law, including freedom of mobility. For example, in 1893, when the twenty-four-year-old Indian lawyer Mohandas Karamchand (later Mahatma) Gandhi booked a first-class seat on a train from Durban to Johannesburg, he expected to arrive safely at his destination. Instead he was thrown off the train when he resisted being moved to a third-class compartment. In 1894, sixty years before Rosa Parks refused to give up her seat in Montgomery, Alabama, Gandhi organized the Natal Indian Congress in South Africa to fight for the rights of people of Indian descent through a policy that in 1896 he called Satyagraha (meaning "truth and firmness"), subsequently called "passive resistance." A decade later in 1904, about twenty miles north of Durban, he helped establish a cooperative farm called "the Phoenix." There, in November 1913, Gandhi led crowds of men, women, and children, including his son, Manilal Gandhi, to resist the imposition of passes on Indians. In 1914, massive demonstrations forced the government to rescind poll taxes on people of South Asian decent and to accept the legality of Hindu and Muslim marriages. Gandhi's son joined him in editing a weekly magazine *Indian Opinion* that Gandhi had founded in 1903. From 1920 to Manilal Gandhi's death in 1956, he published the magazine, taking time off to support his father in the struggle for Indian independence in the 1930s, and participating in the South African Defiance Campaign in 1952.[1] Manilal Gandhi upheld the campaign for democracy through passive resistance in both South Africa and India, where popular forces ousted the British and established an independent state in 1947.[2]

While Mahatma Gandhi and his son and other supporters were fighting against racial discrimination and for civil and political rights for people of Indian descent in South Africa in 1910, the British united their four separate colonies into the Union of South Africa, made it a dominion of the British Empire, and turned over power to whites. Two years later, the African National Congress (ANC), known until 1923 as the National African Land Group, formed to fight against discrimination and to win full civil and political rights for all people in South Africa. That same year, across the Atlantic in Cuba, Afro-Cubans involved in a similar struggle to gain equal democratic rights were massacred for forming the Independent Party of Color.

During the Second World War, in which contrary to the wishes of most Afrikaners and the Nationalist Party, South Africa supported the Allies, black, Asian, and colored people hoped that they might benefit from an Allied victory. In 1943, the ANC, which had long been dominated by highly educated middle-class men, underwent an internal revolution led by the young radicals, Walter Sisulu, Oliver Tambo, and Nelson Mandela. They called for more militant though peaceful acts of civil disobedience to win self-government for people of color.

At about the same time as the youth movement formed in 1943, women—many of whom, like Frances Baard, were factory workers, union activists, and affiliates of the ANC—organized the Women's League to draw masses of women into the struggle. Baard was born in Kimberly near the diamond mines where she gained an education in English and Tswana at a local Methodist school. She lost her teaching job in a rural school during the Second World War, married, and became a factory worker in Port Elizabeth.[3]

During harvest season, she labored as a cannery worker from 6 a.m. to 10 p.m. doing what was considered women's work: peeling, chopping, and seeding the fruit. Although the ANC had earlier ignored women and excluded them from full membership, by the early 1950s, the organization began to realize the importance of mobilizing people in the townships and squatter settlements, and slowly turned to women. Baard and other ANC women went door to door, asking other women for suggestions about how to solve their problems, and then reported the women's complaints and suggestions to ANC meetings, where conversations ranged from local issues to national affairs. Baard began holding small meetings of fellow workers at her home. She recalled that "sometimes during the week about ten people would come to my house. Then somebody . . . would come to talk to us. . . . When we wanted to organize the women too we would call them to our houses in the evening when they had come back from work. Then we would talk to them about things that were wrong and take decisions on these things, the same as at ANC small meetings. We would take the decisions from these meetings to the branch meetings and we would discuss them there. So, from all these meetings, and talking with many people, we learnt many things, and after I had been a member of the ANC for a while I began to understand things much better, and I began to see clearly for myself what is bad and what is good."[4]

Like other supporters of the Allies during the Second World War, ANC members thought that victory over the Nazis would help bring about a transition to democracy in their own country. But their hopes were dashed when the Nationalist Party of Afrikaners came to power in 1948 and coordinated all of the previously diverse systems of discrimination into one national program of Apartheid. In contrast to the United States where segregation never became the official law of the land despite its many advocates in Congress, in postwar South Africa, Apartheid became national policy. The laws categorized people by race and discriminated against people identified as black, colored, and Asian. Only those identified as colored could work in Cape Town and only blacks in Johannesburg. Blacks also predominated in Port Elizabeth and in the townships of New Brighton, eight miles to the north of downtown, but large numbers of Indians continued to live and work there too. Port Elizabeth, a cross between present-day San Francisco and postwar Detroit, was an important shipping, maritime, fruit packing, and industrial center known for its relatively liberal policies. Although blacks, Indians, and Malay blacks were free to go about without passes from the 1930s through the 1950s, they had to observe curfews and were not permitted to go to the same schools, ride the same buses, occupy the same railroad cars and waiting rooms, or stand in the same post office lines as white people. As the Nationalists consolidated their electoral gains and sought to intensify some of the most restrictive local laws, one of the people who fought hardest through the ANC to end discrimination was Frances Baard.

The conversations about democracy in the postwar period roused people like Baard to join unions as a way to win workers' rights. When Ray Alexander, a leader of the South African Food and Cannery Workers' Union, came to Port Elizabeth after the War, Baard and many of her fellow workers embraced the union movement as a means to gain democratic rights as workers. As Baard argued: "We found it was not so difficult to get the workers interested in the trade union because they knew that they were getting very little money, and when the union was telling them that 'If you are united you can fight for more wages,' they knew they must come together to make things better.'" [5] As the organizational secretary of the union committee Baard taught her fellow workers how to act democratically to achieve their goals. "They put up their hands at the meeting, yes they want this strike, or no they don't want it. Maybe they take a decision that we are going to strike if

Frances Baard, longtime South African trade-union and women's leader, addresses a meeting of the United Democratic Front (UDF) in 1983. The UDF, a coalition of religious, social, student, and trade union organizations, formed early in 1983 to insist that the government grant voting rights to the black majority rather than simply provide limited voting rights to so-called mixed-race ("colored") people and those of Indian descent. Paul Weinberg / South Photographs / Africa Media Online

what we want from the employers is not met. . . . We used to try again, try to talk to them because we didn't like strikes because the workers used to be dismissed and some used to be arrested when we went on strike so we always try to talk to the management first. If we have a strike, all the workers would stand outside the factory. Nobody would go in."[6] In effect, union membership forged a new arena for participatory democracy, one that enabled people to formulate strategy and create new rights for themselves and their fellow citizens.

Similarly, people who functioned as partial citizens, by virtue of being colonial subjects of the Allied forces in the Second World War, assumed or demanded that they be elevated to equal citizenship or gain complete independence from their colonizers. India, parts of which had been under some form of British colonialism since the eighteenth century, had been attempting to win home rule and then complete independence as far back as 1885, when the Indian National Congress was formed.

Gandhi arrived back in India in 1914, a hero whose goals and methods were something of a mystery. He saw Indian troops drafted to defend democracy during the First World War and he and the Congress Party fully expected increased independence in the British Commonwealth. But even during the First World War, Gandhi defended striking indigo workers in Bijar, despite British opposition. By 1919, when the war had ended but little had changed for the poorest workers, Gandhi organized a national program of passive resistance.[7] When it was clear that the troops returned to the same conditions they had left, Gandhi continued to help the oppressed and exploited wage campaigns to improve working conditions and eliminate social discrimination through a practice of passive resistance that made the government use force against those who were peacefully demonstrating for their rights. This strategy became a formidable weapon for the achievement of democracy in twentieth-century India, South Africa, and the United States.

For Gandhi and others, such as Muhammad Ali Jinnah, independence from Britain was a necessary goal to permit Indians of all religions, castes, and classes gain rights to choose how to conduct their lives. But Ali Jinnah and Gandhi had different strategies for bringing that about. Ali Jinnah, at first a loyal member of the Congress Party, was the son of a Muslim convert from Hinduism. Like the young Gandhi, Ali Jinnah was educated in Great Britain, trained as a lawyer, adopted British dress, and was at first committed to keeping Hindus and Muslims together in a multi-religious, independent Indian state. But Gandhi's increasing endorsement of social mobilization rather than parliamentary politics, his personal charisma, and his growing impatience with Great Britain's placing its own welfare above that of its colonies drove Ali Jinnah away from the Congress Party to the Muslim League.

From 1940, while the British were fighting the Fascists in Europe and drafting imperial subjects to defend British interests, the British were doing little or nothing to protect their colonies and mandates that were facing Japanese aggression in Asia. In fact, in the spring and summer of 1942, the Japanese armies overran Singapore, Malaya, and Burma (now known as Myanmar) and threatened the northwest Indian region of Assam. Although Indian troops fought alongside the British in Europe, little was done to protect India itself. Gandhi and the Congress Party organized an independence movement known as "Quit India" to drive out the British at the same time that it attempted to protect India from the threat of a Japanese invasion. The British might not have had the troops or the inclination to defend its Asian colonies and protectorates, but it had sufficient investment in India to put down the attempted independence movement by jailing Gandhi's partner and ally Jawaharlal Nehru and other members of the Congress Party. Following victory in the Second World War, however, troops that had incurred heavy losses in Monte Cassino and elsewhere in defense of the Allies presumed that independence would be their reward. Ali Jinnah despaired of any coalition with the Congress Party and, when Britain finally agreed to independence in 1947, the Indian subcontinent was split according to highly unworkable borders. The Punjab in the west and Bengal in the East were partitioned between the Muslim state of

Mahatma Gandhi (right) and Jawaharlal Nehru were longtime allies in the campaign to win Indian independence from Great Britain. Although both pursued democracy and attempted to keep India from being divided along religious lines, Gandhi also tried to promote more spiritual concerns. In 1938, on the eve of the Second World War, he explained that "Democracy of the West is, in my opinion, only so-called. It has germs in it, certainly, of the true type. But it can only come when all violence is eschewed and malpractices disappear. The two go hand in hand. Indeed, malpractice is a species of violence. If India is to evolve the true type, there should be no compromise with violence or untruth." Library of Congress, LC-USZ62-111090

Pakistan and the secular state of India, a process by which over 12 million people crossed the new borders and anywhere from a few hundred thousand to over a million Muslims, Hindus, Parsis, and Sikhs died en route or fell victim to waves of riots and massacres.

Complications spurred by imperialist tendencies in the aftermath of the Second World War in fact added to the discrediting of democratic processes all over the world. Not only were millions of refugees driven from their homes as a result of partition and countless Asians, Arabs, Europeans, and Africans dislocated from places where they had lived for centuries, but millions of Jewish and Roma people, disabled citizens and homosexuals, had been massacred simply to fulfill the racial and eugenic prejudices of warring countries. It soon became clear that those who still believed in democracy would either have to establish procedures and institutions to create new political processes or all hopes for democracy would end for the foreseeable future.

To prevent additional conflicts from arising, to revise the rules of war, and to bring specific perpetrators to justice, the countries that had just won the war attempted to formulate a new system of international law designed to prevent future atrocities of the kind of that had just taken place. The Trial of the Major War Figures before the International Military Tribunal at Nuremberg (1945–46) is by far the most famous. Symbolically, holding the trial in the city the Nazis had used for their large pageants was something of a performance of ritual cleansing. Twenty-one Nazi leaders, including Hermann Goering, Alfred Jodl, and Ernst Kaltenbrunner, were tried and eleven hanged for newly defined "crimes against humanity" that have no statute of limitation since crimes against humanity are considered so odious that they transcend the laws of individual countries. Adolph Hitler and his master of propaganda, Josef Goebbels, had both committed suicide rather than face those who had defeated them and Benito Mussolini had been hung by his heels by the partisans who overthrew him before the Nazis retook parts of Italy. Considered a living god by his people, Japanese Emperor Hirohito was forced to accept a descent in his status, from god to person. Twenty-eight other leaders, including the Japanese prime minister, minister of war, minister of the navy, and various generals, were forced to face trial at which seven of the defendants were sentenced to death and sixteen received life sentences. At Nuremberg, prosecutors, made up of American, French, British, and Russian jurists, brought charges not only against Nazi leaders, but also against journalists and businessmen who had colluded to use slave labor and work to death Jews, Poles, Slavs, and other members of conquered people.

Although some called the trial of the Nazi leaders an example of victor's justice, others agree that the principles laid out in the trials set a standard for democratic justice. This was especially true about the excuse that members of the military should be exonerated because they were "just following orders" when they committed crimes against humanity. The jurists argued that targeting certain races, nationalities, or ethnic groups for extermination was so heinous that they could never be excused by any legal or moral system.

An offshoot of these trials was the creation of the United Nations' Universal Declaration of Human Rights, with the strong influence of Eleanor Roosevelt, and the promulgation of the third phase of the Geneva Convention. The Universal Declaration, especially article 55 of the UN Charter, proclaimed that "the foundation of freedom, justice and peace" lies with "recognition of the equal and inalienable rights of all members of the human family".[8] The plans for the United Nations were first formed during the Second World War at conferences in San Francisco and Dumbarton Oaks in Washington, DC. Having learned from the mistakes of the League of Nations, the newly formed United Nations attempted to create more forceful legislative commissions similar to those of many democratic governments. All member states belonged to the General Assembly that debated particular issues, and the victors in the Second World War, augmented by two rotating representatives of other states, formed a Security Council and standing organizations such as the United Nations Economic, Social, and Cultural Organization, UNESCO, also came into being. The goal was to put the work of international relations on a democratic path.

Some people thought that the transformations in international law and the triumph of the Allies would lay a new path for democratic freedoms. Inspired by India's successful achievement of independence in 1947 and appalled at the reactionary Nationalist Party's electoral victory in South Africa in 1948, the African National Congress's (ANC's) youth group formulated a Program for Action in 1949.[9] The "Program" attempted to win political and civil rights through massive strikes, boycotts, and civil disobedience, pitting the bodies of oppressed people against the military force of the government.

A Nationalist celebration of the three-hundredth anniversary of the Dutch incursion into South Africa on April 6, 1952, provided the occasion for bringing masses of people into the struggle. Seeing an opportunity to challenge the Nationalist legislation, the ANC and the South African Indian Congress decided to attack six particularly egregious laws. The six-month-long Defiance Campaign of 1952 witnessed the

In the wake of the Second World War, the recently formed General Assembly of the United Nations passed the Universal Declaration of Human Rights. The document, written by a committee chaired by Eleanor Roosevelt, demanded the "recognition of the inherent dignity and . . . equal and inalienable rights of all members of the human family" and called for "freedom, justice and peace in the world." United Nations, Photo #117539

arrest of 8,500 people, as the ANC grew from approximately seven thousand to over one hundred thousand members.

In the 1952 Defiance Campaign, the ANC and the Indian National Congress of South Africa singled out laws they believed had been fundamental in transforming South Africa into an Apartheid state. Despite the success of the Defiance Campaign in bringing ordinary Africans into opposition to the government, the Nationalist Party ultimately succeeded in solidifying Apartheid as national law, thus forcing the ANC to take up arms to defeat it. But the struggle that lasted until the 1994 election, which marked a transition to democracy in South Africa by granting equal voting rights for all, actually began in 1952.

Looking back on the six fundamental laws the campaign attacked, it is apparent that they were designed to accomplish exactly the opposite of what they claimed. For instance, the Bantu Authorities Act of 1951 supposedly granted moderate rights of self-government under black leadership to Africans in certain areas, but, along with the Stock Limitation law, the Bantu Authorities Act drove many black men and women off their land and transformed them into migrant laborers. In turn, the Separate Representation of Voters Act of 1951 robbed the so-called colored voters even of their previous right to elect white legislators to represent their interests in Parliament. And the Suppression of Communism Act of 1950 attempted to preclude any opposition to the government by defining all dissent as "communist."[10]

By far, the most important laws the Defiance Campaign attacked were those that intensified the use of passes. For example, the Population and Registration Act of 1950, although at first glance designed to divide and conquer by classifying everyone by race—as natives, Asians, colored, or whites—actually united many of the groups by forcing all non-white men to carry passes. Supplemented in the first days of the Defiance Campaign by the Orwellian July 1952 "Abolition of Passes and Co-ordination of Documents Act," the Population and Registration law also intensified attempts to force women of color to join men of color in carrying passes. These complemented the Group Areas Act of 1950 (another of the six targeted laws) that forbade blacks and coloreds from living in certain places for more than seventy-two hours without passes and assigned others to certain neighborhoods, cities, and regions. The government also set up a system by which people who agreed to carry passes could gain temporary residence in order to get medical treatment for ailing relatives or special education for children. Once a person accepted a pass, however, he or she was like a parolee and had to report regularly to an official. Having one's movements monitored made people susceptible to constant surveillance and made changing jobs or houses nearly impossible.[11]

Nelson Mandela, a lawyer and Deputy President of the ANC in 1952, led the Campaign of Defiance of Unjust Laws that attempted to use mass mobilization to end Apartheid. He was joined by countless unsung heroes. The campaign began with a letter from the ANC and the Indian National Congress asking the Prime Minister to rescind the six unjust laws by February 29, 1952. He refused. Demonstrations followed on April 6, during the anniversary of the Dutch landing, and, on June 1, 1952, J. S. Moroka, the ANC President, announced that the Defiance Campaign against Apartheid would begin on June 26, 1952, later designated as South African Freedom Day.[12] During the campaign that lasted roughly from June to December 1952 and continued with sporadic demonstrations in early 1953, mass meetings attracted groups as large as 15,000 in Johannesburg, 10,000 in Cape Town, and nearly 20,000 in Port Elizabeth and East Brighton, where urban Black workers and lower-middle-class people of Indian descent committed themselves to rescinding the most repressive laws.

Even before the Defiance Campaign, Florence Matomela of the ANC's Women's League had already spent time in prison for her role in the Port Elizabeth anti-pass demonstrations of 1950, when she was jailed for six weeks for violating curfews, going into sections forbidden to blacks, and for leading a group of people in burning their pass books. The mother of nine children of whom only five survived infancy, Matomela, like Francis Baard, was trained as a teacher, but was unable to exercise her profession. Instead, she, like Baard, became a community leader, who helped the ANC mobilize migrant workers to fight for democratic reforms in racial relations through mass demonstrations.[13]

Another resister, Annie Silinga, hailed from Transkei and migrated to Cape Town in 1937 to join her husband after four of their children died because of insufficient food and medical care. In 1948 she joined the Langa Vigilance Association outside of Cape Town. Silinga's lack of a formal education did not prevent her from becoming a founder in 1954 of the Federation of South African Women (FEDSAW), a multiracial women's group that organized against the imposition of passes for women. Silinga's prominence as a leader resulted in the government's banishing her to her birthplace in 1955 for repeated efforts to resist carrying a pass. Unwilling to abandon her home and family, she secretly returned to Langa and successfully appealed to have her residency legalized. A year later she was imprisoned again and accused of treason. She was exonerated, became head of the ANC Women's League in Cape Town, was imprisoned again in 1960, and remained active in politics until her death.[14]

Annie Silinga, Florence Matomela, Frances Baard, and Nelson Mandela all began their careers as democratic leaders in the postwar period, but their lives were shaped by the Defiance Campaign, a massive effort to broaden public awareness of what was transpiring in South Africa. Like the Civil Rights movement that followed it in the United States, the Defiance Campaign attracted the attention of the world media to the repression of democratic rights taking place in South Africa. The ANC mobilized tens of thousands of people who chose to remain in jail rather than pay bail, and challenged the resources of the government that was ill-equipped to feed and house so many people. Commenting on South African events occurring barely six years after India had gained its independence, the Indian National Congress called the Defiance Campaign a "satyagraha" in the spirit of Mahatma Gandhi, and accused the South African government of violating the laws of civilized countries. Although the Defiance Campaign can be said to have had limited success, during 1952 and early 1953 more than 74,000 people were prosecuted for violating the pass laws, an indication of passive resistance in its own right.[15]

The Defiance Campaign marked the beginning, not the end, of an extensive movement for democracy, and in 1954, six months before Rosa Parks refused to give up her seat on the bus in Montgomery, Alabama, the ANC, meeting in a field in Kliptown near Johannesburg, began shaping a People's Charter, an alternative constitution that three-thousand black, Indian, colored, and white delegates formulated during two days on June 25 and 26, 1955. Like the American Constitution, the Charter located the idea of national sovereignty in a generalized group called "the people," and proclaimed that "the people shall govern." The charter also made economic claims that the land should belong to those who cultivate it and that all citizens should share the national wealth.[16]

Nelson Mandela, who was under banning orders that forbade his participation in any political meetings, secretly attended the Kliptown meeting. In his autobiography, *Long Walk to Freedom*, he claimed that the charter was "a mixture of practical goals and poetic language. It extol[led] the abolition of racial discrimination and the achievement of equal rights for all. It welcome[d] all who embrace freedom to participate in the making of a democratic, nonracial South Africa. It captured the hopes and dreams of the people and acted as a blueprint for the liberation struggle and the future of the nation."[17] The government retaliated, charging thirty-five ANC members with "communism" in September 1952.[18] Then in 1955 the government orchestrated a Treason Trial against 156 people involved with the Freedom Charter.[19] Despite the repression associated with the five-year-long trial, the struggle continued in the streets and unions of South Africa.

From 1943, when the ANC's Women's League fought alongside men to liberate all South African citizens to the unsuccessful 1956 to 1959 campaign of the Federation of South African Women to resist imposition of passes on them, South African women chanted "Now you have touched the women, you have struck a rock, you have dislodged a boulder, you will be crushed." Using some of the strategies of passive resistance pioneered in the Defiance Campaign, women marched on city halls and petitioned mayors and city council members all over South Africa to defend their freedom of movement. Then they gathered 100,000 signatures on a petition that 20,000 women tried to present to the Prime Minister on August 9, 1956, protesting against laws mandating them to carry passes. The Federation continued to resist largely through the local organizations that mobilized in factories and in the townships, attempting to overcome the threat of unemployment or lack of medical care for their children if they failed to carry passes. Although the government ultimately prevailed in 1959 and 1960, legions of women learned to organize local women's councils to defend themselves through the remaining long nightmare of Apartheid.

Far away, in Montgomery, Alabama, Rosa Parks studied to become a hero. She had attended segregated schools, which, though lacking resources, had teachers, who themselves had benefited from the commitment of black leaders, some of whom were emancipated slaves. Following high school, Parks married a barber and worked as a seamstress. She never stopped reading, studying, and meeting with others in the black community. In 1955, Rosa Parks attended the Highlander Folk School in the mountains of Tennessee to gain the training she needed in the tactics of nonviolent resistence.

The Highlander Folk School, founded in the 1930s by Myles Horton, a poor White southerner, was a pioneering social institution in which the ideas of nonviolent resistance blended with incipient notions of citizenship education to create a new image of democracy.[20] Highlander gathered people to promote social change by teaching them to empower themselves and those around them. Working first with poor farmers, craftsmen, and laborers, the school became a place where incipient trade union organizers met to discuss developing the capacity of future leaders. On December 1, 1955, three months after Rosa Parks studied history and the tactics others had employed to gain full citizenship rights, she found the courage to stay in her seat on the Cleveland Avenue bus and thus became a central figure in the yearlong Montgomery Bus Boycott.

A less well-known leader, JoAnn Robinson, a professor of English at Alabama State College, first envisioned resistance in the name of democratic change more than a year earlier.[21] Robinson, on her way home to Cleveland to visit her family for Christmas, sat in the first seat she found on a nearly empty bus in Montgomery. The White bus driver stopped the bus and ordered her to move to the back. She fled, but on May 21, 1954, a year and a half before Rosa Parks refused to move, JoAnn Robinson wrote to the mayor of Montgomery demanding "improved conditions for black riders" and threatened a bus boycott.[22]

Another of Rosa Parks's allies, E. D. Nixon of the Brotherhood of Sleeping Car Porters, the largest and most militant union of African Americans in the country, had worked for years backstage, helping to choreograph resistance to segregation. Nixon had grown up in Montgomery and became one of the main spokesmen for the Black community there. A. Philip Randolph, the president of Nixon's union, had pioneered the use of mass mobilization to demand the end of lynching, the achievement of equal wages for Negro men and women, and desegregation of the armed forces. As early as 1944, Nixon had already established his own political credentials and led nearly 800 black men to the polls to vote in Alabama. At the same time he became a leader of the NAACP, an officer of the Progressive Democratic Club, and later helped found the Montgomery Improvement Association.[23] He was aware of every leaf that fell in the black community in Montgomery, and for several years, Nixon and other local black activists had been eager to put an end to segregation. Rosa Parks, the well-known local leader of the Youth Division of the NAACP and a respectable married woman who had already worked as E. D. Nixon's secretary in the state-wide NAACP office, was just the person to serve.[24]

The segregation laws in Montgomery mandated that the first ten seats on city buses were reserved for whites and the back seats for blacks, with three or four rows in the middle in which blacks could sit until whites arrived. Mrs. Parks had just sat down in an aisle seat just behind the whites section in one of the middle rows, when the bus filled up.[25] Gradually blacks around her gave up their seats, but the four black passengers, including Mrs. Parks, kept sitting when the bus driver first ordered them to move. Even when the other three got up, Mrs. Parks stayed in her seat. The driver stopped the bus just opposite the Empire Theater, went to a pay phone, and called the police, who took her to the local police station and booked her. She called her mother, who called Parks's husband, who got in touch with Nixon who went to bail out Rosa Parks.

Black people had a lot to fear from prison, and respectable, church-going black people raised their children to avoid any contact with the police. Though the movement would later utilize mass detention as a tactic of passive resistance, at first Parks had no crowd of supporters urging her on. The real question was whether she had the will and the strength to lead a movement, and she did.

Nixon, the consummate political organizer, then decided that there should be a mass meeting at a downtown church to assure that middle-class black professionals and business leaders would attend. He called the recently appointed twenty-six-year-old minister of the Dexter Avenue Baptist Church, Martin Luther King Jr., and asked if they could meet at his church on Friday, December 2, 1955. Nixon then called Ralph Abernathy and dozens of other ministers to get their support. The day after Rosa Parks was arrested, Robinson and her organization, the Montgomery Women's Political Council, the black alternative to the locally segregated League of Women Voters, composed, printed, and distributed flyers calling on the black community of Montgomery to boycott all the buses on Monday.[26]

On Monday, December 5, Rosa Parks was tried and found guilty of violating Alabama's Segregation Laws and went home on bail. Nixon, Abernathy, and another minister started planning the mass meeting and discussed hiring black bus drivers for black neighborhoods, seating people on a first-come, first-serve basis, and calling for more courteous treatment of all passengers—hardly unreasonable demands. Then Nixon and the ministers named their organization the Montgomery Improvement Association (MIA). Nixon suggested that King, who was new in town, be named as director.[27] King gave a rousing speech on December 2, launching the Montgomery Improvement Association, which was supported by Montgomery's sixty-eight black social, labor, fraternal, political, and economic organizations that preexisted the boycott.[28]

The Montgomery struggle has gone down in history as the first stage of the Civil Rights Movement, and participating in the boycott became a means of creating a new collective identity as well as gaining certain specific democratic rights. Although the main leaders, apart from JoAnn Robinson and Rosa Parks, were men, the mass base of foot soldiers who spilled out into the streets were women, who challenged segregation in the form of the largely empty buses that rolled through the streets of Montgomery, causing the Metropolitan Transit Company that ran the buses to lose $3,000 a day during the boycott.[29]

A boycott, like other forms of passive resistance, is anything but passive. Successfully resisting unjust authority often convinces people of their ability to act collectively to govern themselves in the future. By lowering people's fear of police and soldiers, boycotts sometimes liberate people to generate democratic demands. Although the Montgomery Improvement Association began with fairly limited goals, its ability to stay together despite consistent repression gave Montgomery's black community courage to continue. Indeed, boycotts demonstrate the power of those that appear to be weak. By withholding contact—by not purchasing specific goods and services and not engaging with those who oppress them—demonstrators reveal their own economic and social power.

Those who demanded integrated busing in Montgomery achieved something more than riding in comfort. The demonstrators had shown that ordinary people could sustain a mass movement and maintain their own dignity despite the violence that defenders of the old order could muster. Although the Montgomery Bus Boycott merely began the campaign for full citizenship by questioning one undemocratic practice, they joined campaigns for democracy that had been sweeping the world following the Second World War.

The Montgomery Bus Boycott and the Defiance Campaign in Port Elizabeth were training grounds in democratic practice. Participants learned to listen to others and formulate their own arguments. The Montgomery Improvement Association drew on the sixty-eight black organizations that preceded it. Those organizations, though not all dedicated to democratic transformation, taught people how to formulate arguments about how to overcome discrimination and repression. Likewise in Port Elizabeth, the ability of the ANC Youth and Women's Leagues to unite labor and neighborhood activists to develop their knowledge about how their individual situation fit into the larger picture created cadres of ordinary people who were able to fight for democratic changes over forty years of resistance to Apartheid. In the streets, congresses, and meetings for self-education, people developed the skills to decide what democracy should mean and how they hoped they would be able to achieve it.

CHAPTER 7

Optimism and Outrage in Struggles for Democracy

Since both the First and Second World Wars had been fought in the name of democracy, and since many of the countries dominated by the Soviet Union after 1945 had been renamed "democratic republics," the very term "democracy" might have seemed questionable in the postwar period. The German philosopher Theodor Adorno claimed that "to write poetry after Auschwitz is barbaric,"[1] and others might argue that all hopes for democracy were futile. Yet, with few if any alternative visions, a rebirth in struggles for democracy and an increasing emphasis on youthful responsibility for righting the wrongs that had led to such conflagrations re-emerged at the end of the Second World War.

Part of the changing times in the United States, as well as in other countries, involved the vast expansion of higher education. Increases in student enrollment in the United States began with the GI Bill of Rights (officially named "The Servicemen's Readjustment Act"), which enabled more than a million veterans (overwhelmingly male) to gain a government-sponsored college or technical education after 1947. And the numbers increased astronomically along with the national birthrate. The baby boomers amounted to 76 million people born between 1946 and 1964, and they accounted for doubling the number of college students in the United States from 3.7 million to 7.8 million between 1960 and 1969.[2] In the immediate postwar period, the older and more experienced veterans set a serious tone for American higher education, especially in their interest in foreign affairs.

The baby boomers shared a sense that, unlike their parents and grandparents, they were on the threshold of a whole new world. In fact, student representatives from communist and capitalist countries and some of their former colonies, gathered in Prague in 1946 to form the International Union of Students, dedicated to bringing young people together in the postwar period. But, when the Soviet Union overthrew the democratic government of Czechoslovakia in 1948, the National Student Association of the United States withdrew from the International Union of Students and surreptitiously began taking funds from the Central Intelligence Agency (CIA).[3] The idea that students were any less pawns in the power struggle between East and West than their parents were proved to be a lie. Nevertheless, the sheer increase in the numbers of students outside the direct control and influence of their families, even in Europe where university attendance increased more slowly, changed the course of history in the 1960s.

Secular and religious universities had long occupied a special place as sanctuaries from the political realm. Until the postwar period, few working-class or even lower-middle-class people attended such institutions in Europe or North America, but colleges and universities nevertheless served as free spaces in which a small number of people from different classes and ethnic groups were able to mingle. In the United States and Europe, most Ivy League, Big Ten, or ancient universities like Oxford, Cambridge, or the Sorbonne entirely excluded or had tiny quotas for everyone but white men from the upper classes. In Africa, where white and black Africans seldom attended the same institutions of higher education, different religious denominations established colleges for black Africans and various Asian groups. Some (but few) students from India attended British institutions of higher learning before India and Pakistan gained their independence in 1947. But Delhi University, founded in 1922, provided a free education to tens of thousands of undergraduates, and the founding of Jawaharlal Nehru University (in 1969) and the expansion in 1973 of the Delhi University to include the South Campus for graduate studies in the Humanities and Social Sciences increased the number of Indian students able to attend college and graduate school.

Students and young workers were also increasingly mobile. From Algeria, Turkey, the Caribbean, India, Pakistan, South Africa, and the German Democratic Republic (GDR or East Germany), young people in large numbers set out in search for jobs or educational institutions that provided sunnier futures. For instance, between 1950 and 1988, 24.5 million largely young people from all of these countries migrated to the Federal Republic of Germany (BRD or West Germany), another 21.9 million people migrated to France, and 25 million more to Switzerland, Scandinavia, Holland, Belgium, and Luxemburg.[4] Living in slums, but with increased disposable income for themselves, these men and smaller number of women were able to read newspapers, debate controversial ideas, and challenge many of the precepts they had been taught in their countries of birth.

Those who stayed home also developed new values and aspirations. In the postwar, middle-class world of Western Europe and the United States, youth came of age. Their parents had waged war, but they were the beneficiaries of peace and prosperity. There was a tendency among the white middle class to be oblivious to widespread international regional wars, racial oppression, and cracks in the social systems of their countries. Yet young people in East Germany could not ignore the oppressive system under which they worked. In April 1953 the government announced increased work quotas and workers throughout East Germany including East Berlin reacted angrily, sometimes slowing down or even striking for short periods. But on June 16, 1953, youthful construction workers, followed by metal workers, mobilized in large numbers in the Russian sector of Berlin. The next day, a large group of supporters among steel workers and miners from the areas of East Germany closest to East Berlin also decided to take action. As Cajo Brendel, a contemporary Dutch commentator reported a few weeks later, 12,000 steel workers of Henningsdorf from nearly thirteen miles outside of East Berlin, "marched arm in arm on a wide front. They came down the road which led from the north, still wearing their work clothes, and with their protective spectacles still hanging around their necks. . . ." [and] "there were women amongst them wearing light shoes . . . which weren't meant for heavy use like this. When their feet began to hurt, the women took off their shoes [and] continued barefoot at no price were they going to be left behind. They were pushed [forward] by a common desire and a common purpose. . . .[5]" Outraged by worsening living conditions and unreasonable factory quotas, the workers and their families launched protests that quickly spread throughout the entire country calling for economic reforms and free elections in the German Democratic Republic.[6] Though brutally repressed within a few days, many of the factory workers managed to organize workers' councils to guide their actions. The uprising indicated that masses of East Germans were deeply dissatisfied with the conditions under which they were forced to live and were willing to risk everything to change them. One factory worker admitted that "It was disastrous that there were no Organization, or anything like that . . . in our area, we were all people who had never gone on strike before. It was all improvised. We had no linkups with any other towns or factories. We didn't know where to begin. But we were totally full of joy that things were happening as they were. All you saw in the crowd [were] faces beaming with emotion because everyone was feeling at last the hour has come, we're freeing ourselves from the yoke of slavery."[7] On the second day of the protest the demonstrators were violently repressed by the East German police and Soviet troops that had been sent in to help quell the uprising. At the end of the day, between 55– and 125 people lay dead, over 1,800 injured, 5,000 or more arrested, and 1,200 sent to prison camps. And yet, the governemnt made June 17 an official holiday in rememberance of the uprising and German unification, and the day was long remembered for the willingness of workers to stand up and demand their rights as citizens.

Scarcely a year after the East German workers asserted their will to be free, American democracy won a major victory when on May 17, 1954, The Supreme Court in *Brown v. the Board of Education of Topeka* outlawed segregation in the public schools. Thurgood Marshall, the chief attorney for the NAACP (The National Association for the Advancement of Colored People), argued the case and not only insisted that separate was never equal, but persuaded the court that, in the words of Chief Justice Earl Warren "[S]egregation [in public education] is a denial of the equal protection of the laws." Accepting psychological as well as legal arguments Marshall had put forward, the court argued that separating some children "from others of similar age and qualifications solely because of their race generates a feeling of inferiority as to their status in the community that may affect their hearts and minds in a way unlikely ever to be undone."

The Kansas court had introduced and the Supreme Court had recognized a psychological dimension to democratic theory when it argued that the "Segregation of white and colored children in public schools has a detrimental effect upon the colored children. The impact is greater when it has the sanction of the law; for the policy of separating the races is usually interpreted as denoting the inferiority of the negro group. A sense of inferiority affects the motivation of a child to learn. Segregation with the sanction of law, therefore, has a tendency to [retard] the educational and mental development of negro children and to deprive them of some of the benefits they would receive in a racial[ly] integrated school." Summing up, Warren wrote: "We conclude that in the field of public education the doctrine of 'separate but equal' has no place. Separate educational facilities are inherently unequal. . . . segregation [in public education] is a denial of the equal protection of the laws."[8] But despite the ruling in favor of desegregation, the law faced resistance and still needed to be implemented.

Students from traditional Black Colleges led the way in turning law into practice. From the courts, they moved to integrating lunch counters in Greensboro, North Carolina, to riding interstate buses on whose highways and in whose waiting rooms civil rights activists put their bodies on the line. Civil rights activists fought to occupy public spaces, until they finally won the right to exercise their votes like other citizens of the United States, rights that were supported by the Voting Right Act of 1965. The Civil Rights Movement transformed the United States for the better between 1954 and 1968, although much work remained even after it was over. In Latin America, similar attempts to expand democracy were also occurring. The 1959 Cuban Revolution raised hope around the region that democratic rights could be broadened and maintained. Young people of both genders had come of age and began to demonstrate their opposition to the great powers, East and West. As singer Bob Dylan observed, "The times they [were] a-changin'."

Democracy, with its multiple meanings all indicating greater personal and collective freedom of choice, remained fragile despite multiple reforms made in its name. In West Germany, in late June 1966, students from SDS (The German Socialist Student Association) occupied space outside the University Senate meeting hall of the Free University of Berlin and expressed their desire that "decisions affecting students be made democratically and with student participation. . . ." They explained that they were mostly interested in "dismantling oligarchic rule and implementing democratic freedom in all areas of society."[9] But when a year later SDS organized a peaceful demonstration protesting a visit to West Germany of the Shah of Iran, who was widely believed to be torturing and executing large numbers of political prisoners, the German police staged a rampage against demonstrators and killed a student in the process. All over West Germany, but especially in Frankfurt and Berlin, students demonstrated for a month in protest against police brutality. As a result, the chief of police and the mayor of Berlin were forced to resign. Students moved from merely demonstrating, to organizing their own classes, and developed their own criticisms of the direction that postwar German society was taking. Further repression of students' demonstrations led to an assassination attempt on April 19 against the leader of SDS, Rudi Dutschke, who lived but never fully recovered from his injuries. The increased violence directed at the students only reinforced their sense that German authoritarianism was intensifying. The government's decision to grant the executive branch extraordinary power during so-called times of emergency, effectively permitting the use of force without the consultation of the legislature—the same kind of emergency powers that Hitler had used to come to power in Nazi Germany—horrified students and members of German trade unions, who organized demonstrations of upwards of 80,000 protesters.[10]

In Czechoslovakia, press censorship began to diminish and constraints on innovation became looser. Beginning in February and March 1968, activists began debating how Marxism might be liberated from Stalinism. At the same time, Czech workers began to form workers' councils in their factories in the spring of 1968.[11] Under the rule of Alexander Dubček, first secretary of the Communist Party, young writers and artists such as Václav Havel produced plays, generated films and paintings, and contributed to what has been called the Prague Spring. Hável's work, which sometimes featured the absurdity of repetitively carrying out orders that made no sense highlighted his notions about politics. As he said: "Genuine politics—even politics worthy of the name—the only politics I am willing to devote myself to—is simply a matter of serving those around us: serving the community and serving those who will come after us. Its deepest roots are moral because it is a responsibility expressed through action, to and for the whole."[12]

Because the Soviets thought that Czechoslovakia had gone too far toward political and intellectual independence, they organized troop maneuvers in mid-June, which led to the diminution of press freedom and a reduction in political debate. When this failed, 165,000 troops from the Warsaw Pact of the Soviet Bloc invaded Czechoslovakia on August 21, 1968, and re-established what they considered to be the proper political order. Despite the invasion, some workers' councils continued to meet surreptitiously until early 1969 when they were more forcefully suppressed. Yet, in Prague and Pilsen, workers demanded the right to make major decisions about how factories should be run.[13] And increasingly, from the sixties through the close of the century, innovative democratic movements attempted to overthrow oppressive governments in order to create more democratic societies. They also applied democratic principles in service of saving the environment, especially as they affected growing regional conflicts over water and fights for the control of natural resources.

It remains to be seen why 1968 was a year when people in so many nations were able to take a stand and alter international trajectories. During a period of massive population growth and one of the greatest expansions of capitalism in history, some people were left behind. Coupled with the contradictions of work and educational possibilities in the richest countries were the continued constraints on self-determination and independence in many former colonies in Africa, Asia, and Latin America. One issue that sparked the events of 1968 was the January Tet Offensive in Vietnam that revealed that few people in South Vietnam were willing to fight to defend their government.

Vietnam, which had fought against Chinese invasions for over four centuries, fell into the French sphere of influence between 1858 and 1883, when the French government under Napoleon III seized power in what later became North Vietnam. By the early twentieth century, a liberation movement had begun to fight sporadically against various puppet governments in order to create more egalitarian societies. Ho Chi Minh, the son of a former civil servant in the French imperial government, became a socialist after the First World War in hopes of bringing about massive social change in his country. But having failed to win the reforms he had hoped for he allied in 1930 with neighbors in Laos and Cambodia to form the Indochinese Communist Party to rid the region of its French rulers. When the Second World War broke out, Ho and his allies fought against Japanese invaders, the French army, and Chinese nationalists. Toward the end of the war, he attempted to negotiate with the antifascist French forces and the United States, but his demands for Vietnamese independence under a Communist regime were rejected. Although the French had, in fact, agreed to withdraw from the northern part of Vietnam after the Second World War, their troop buildup in the south led to war from 1946 until the French were finally driven out in the battle of Dien Bien Phu in 1954. Even after the French retreat, the country remained divided, with the United States supporting the South Vietnamese forces. By 1959 a second war, known as the Vietnam War, began and lasted until 1975, when a final peace treaty was signed.

The Vietnam War generated photographs and TV footage that revealed a level of violence and environmental devastation that shocked people around the world. Photographs of naked children being burnt alive by the gelled petroleum called napalm and South Vietnamese officers shooting captives as if they were merely wooden ducks in a shooting gallery provoked some people to try to stop the violence. Ironically, French students were among those who were most moved. The French, having handed over the anticommunist forces of South Vietnam to American advisors in 1954, seemed especially responsible for what transpired later on.

The combination of frustration over Vietnam coupled with the seeming failures of French universities to provide training for meaningful lives contributed to dashing hopes for democracy in the late 1960s in France. Students who were the first in their families to attend college were often sorely disappointed. The curricula that they were required to study seemed increasingly irrelevant. No one would have predicted that a controlled and nearly quiescent industrial working class would ally with students, immigrant workers, and technocrats to challenge the government of President Charles de Gaulle in May and early June 1968. French students enrolled in classes in which the student-teacher ratio amounted to 200 to 1, and the curriculum, designed to incorporate elites into societies they would rule, proved inadequate to prepare ordinary students to earn a living in the modern world. The French government that controlled the curriculum and dictated who would get jobs did not seem to have space for self-governing institutions through which workers and students might express their own goals and desires.

Daniel Cohn-Bendit—who became known as Danny the Red (or Communist)—was one of the students whose image of reform rested on views of popular democracy. Cohn-Bendit, the child of Jewish parents who had fled Nazi Germany to settle in France, was born in France in 1945 and remained there after his parents returned to Germany. He enrolled in Nanterre, one of France's new universities built among the tenements that housed industrial workers, including temporary immigrants known as "guest workers" from Italy, Portugal, Spain, and Algeria. Nanterre and its cousin universities, Vincennes and the ancient Sorbonne, lacked the facilities or teaching staff to educate the number of students they admitted. In fact, enrollments at French universities had tripled from 170,000 to 514,000 or higher between 1958 and 1968.[14]

Inchoate dissatisfaction among European and American students came to a head with North Vietnam's Tet Offensive in January 1968 Demonstrations of the National Vietnam Committee at Nanterre led to student arrests and protests in March 1968.[15]

In many countries, small groups of young people believed that unimpeded military action and inadequate university educations threatened human rights and democracy. West German students, the only group in Europe to have undergone intense de-Nazification programs following World War II, demanded that their parents and grandparents confess their complicity with the Nazis.[16] French students and intellectuals, in turn, demanded a full accounting of Vichy France's colaboration with the Nazis. On March 29, 1968, just short of twenty-three years after the end of the Second World War, the dean of the Sorbonne called in the police to quash peaceful student demonstrators who were demanding university reforms. In the following month, up to 500 students and a handful of their professors organized into study groups to discuss the nature of French education and its relationship to French politics. Dissatisfaction with working and living conditions intensified, especially among young male and female workers in textile and auto plants.

Following the attempted assassination of the German student leader Rudi Dutschke on April 19, 1968, thousands of French students protested, leading Cohn-Bendit and five other students to be arrested for being rabble-rousers. After another series of student demonstrations, the dean of faculty at Nanterre temporarily closed the university on May 2, 1968. Escalating the violence, university administrators called in the riot police, who arrested students indiscriminately. When fighting broke out, the administrators closed the university for the first time since June 1940, when the Nazis invaded France. Subsequent hearings and demonstrations led to pitched battles, barricades, the arrest of more than 400 students, and hundreds of injuries on both sides.[17]

Strikes and demonstrations swept the country and more moderate French people turned on the government in defense of the college students. Workers and students throughout France took up the cause, calling for decentralization and democratic councils of students and workers to run the universities and the factories. On May 10, the struggle escalated and five thousand high school students joined with tens of thousands of university students to occupy the Latin Quarter around the Sorbonne, erecting—à la the French Revolution—more than sixty barricades. The police, not content with tear gas and hand grenades, turned to using poison gas and sexually molesting women activists.[18]

By Monday, May 13, tens of thousands of French workers had left their jobs and 200,000 to 600,000 demonstrators inundated Paris. Most of the six Renault factories, including Boulogne Billancourt, the largest auto plant in France, with a labor force of 35,000 workers, closed down, though many workers occupied the plants. At first, the largely Communist labor leaders opposed the insurrection and spoke out against the students, but they ultimately followed their members' lead. Immigrants from North Africa, Yugoslavia, and Portugal worked in some of the auto plants and were reluctant to forfeit the wages that their impoverished families back home depended upon. Yet even they walked off the job and honored the strike. A few days later, the union

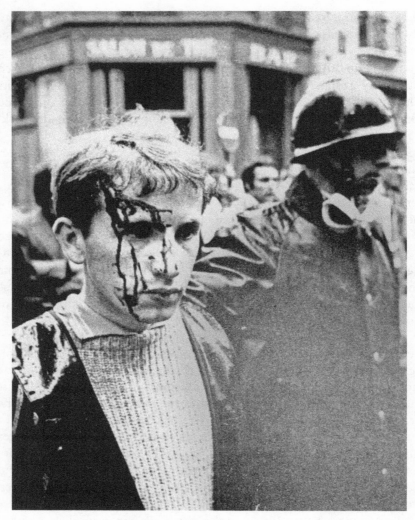

In 1968, student uprisings all over the world were violently suppressed when they demanded an end to the Vietnam War and the democratization of their own governments. Universities were closed and students faced riot police who were often out of control. The repression of students in Paris outraged unionized workers, who nearly overthrew the government of Charles de Gaulle. In the course of struggle, students and workers tried to work out new democratic governmental structures. A French student explained how his group called "for the creation of student power, whether this goes to the union or to the strike committee. What is important today is to develop the struggle according to proposals which the students themselves decide on. . . ." These included "release and amnesty for the demonstrators, police withdrawal, faculty reopening. . . . But what produced the result was action; not that we succeeded by force, but that we won politically; the population was with us. That is what forced the government to give way." AP Photo/Guy Kopelowicz of television workers attempted to rid the media of government control. Within a week, print journalists joined in and claimed rights to help edit headlines and news content.[19] Once the state had bared its iron hand, it could no longer deny the repression that permeated every aspect of contemporary life.

Students and teachers throughout France, especially in Lyons, Paris, Nantes, and Normandy, formed local councils to design and execute educational reforms and invited students to participate in decision-making. Auto and aeronautical workers, ship-builders, postal workers, air traffic controllers, and others all over the country went out on strike on May 17. At the same time students joined workers and closed all six Renault factories, including the one in Paris. Silk-screening cooperatives were formed at the School of Fine Arts, preparing posters proclaiming commodities as "the opium of the people" and calling for the imposition of "The general will against the will of the general." They added that it was "forbidden to forbid" and called on the public to "be realistic. Demand the impossible." The actors' union declared the right to determine what plays their companies would perform. Practically every large auditorium was filled with students, debating about how to humanize their lives and how to improve their educational system.

By May 21, ten to twelve million workers were on strike, far beyond the three million who belonged to unions. On May 24 President de Gaulle spoke on radio and television, promising a referendum, but the following day police shot and wounded over 500 people and arrested nearly 800 demonstrators. On May 27, militant workers negotiated a ten percent pay increase, but young workers wanted more, and strikes continued to spread. According to at least one account, the government paid its supporters to go to the Place de la Concord and chant "Cohn-Bendit to Dachau," and "Students to the gas ovens."[20] Unable to quash demonstrators by any other means, on May 29 de Gaulle called in tanks. Then he organized new elections and offered workers contracts for higher wages. By June 5 most strikes and occupations had come to a halt, but some refused to settle until the government agreed to create more workers' committees to control the factories and schools. The government, seeking to punish those who had resisted its dictates, deported many immigrants on June 9. Boycotting the elections, younger workers and students failed to challenge de Gaulle at the polls on June 23 and 30 and he easily won re-election. Without more coordinated action and the formation of student and worker councils to consolidate the victories won in specific factories and university campuses, the movement could not create the stable institutions necessary to exercise their democratic rights.

The issue of state violence also brought increasing numbers of students, workers, farmers, and other citizens into the streets in Mexico in the late summer and fall of 1968. Like Paris, Mexico City had embarked on widespread urban renewal to accommodate a growing population. Between 1960 and 1965, the Mexican government sponsored the creation of a satellite city known as Nonoalco-Tlatelolco consisting of schools, hospitals, stores, and over a hundred high-rise apartment buildings accommodating 70,000 people. The complex was divided into three parts with separate buildings for wealthy, middle-class, and modest families, who were supposed to enjoy the parks, gardens, and wall murals surrounding their living quarters.

Democracy can only flourish when citizens are confident that those responsible for maintaining order will deal with all citizens in a responsible manner. That was anything but the case in the months leading up to the October 1968 Olympics in Mexico. The government, which for all of the forty or more years since the end of the Mexican Revolution had been governed by the Institutional Revolutionary Party (PRI), was especially nervous about social disorder and eager to suppress dissent that might tarnish Mexico's image on the eve of the Olympics. As the first Latin American country to host the Olympics and as a country intensely eager for more foreign investment and tourism, and increasingly fearful of crime and social unrest, the Mexican government had increased its police forces adding special units of riot police. The government also deployed army troops to deal with minimally threatening groups such as unruly high school and college students. Police violence became associated with those charged with maintaining the peace. As the Olympics drew nearer, outbreaks of violence and social discontent increased.

Student demonstrations seemed to incite the special ire of the armed police and military, and the National and city governments consistently supported the use of force. On July 25, 1968, high school students demonstrating against police brutality intersected a march celebrating the anniversary of the Cuban Revolution, and violence ensued, leading to arrests of various communist activists and student demands that the police chief be fired.[21] The police attacks escalated at the end of July as they fired on and wounded demonstrating high school students and invaded the headquarters of the National Autonomous University of Mexico (UNAM). To effectively counter the police and the armed forces and to assure that democratic decision-making could take place, students formed a National Strike Committee (CNH).[22] The students demanded the disbanding of the riot police, the establishment of the right to strike, the liberation of political prisoners, political freedom, and changing the penal code to protect free speech.[23] On August 13, the students from the National Polytechnical Institute (IPM) called for university strikes and demonstrations in the Zócalo (Mexico City's symbolic central plaza, which dates back to the Aztecs and early Spanish colonial rulers) unless the police investigated the killing and injuries of the student demonstrators. Two hundred and fifty thousand people gathered in the square and called for democracy, by which they meant that the voice of the people organized in local committees would prevail. Equal numbers congregated in the plaza in the subsequent weeks that led up to August 27.[24] That night the crowd supposedly doubled to half a million outside the National Palace as students, workers, and engaged citizens showed their displeasure with the government.[25] Mobilizations took place throughout September and October largely around the right to demonstrate and demands for the liberation of political prisoners who were jailed, tortured, and even "disappeared." The government denied the presence of political prisoners and then reversed itself and offered to free the prisoners once the protesters withdrew. Then on September 18, dissatisfied with the continued mobilization of the National Strike Committee, the head of security ordered the army to take over UNAM's campus and arrest hundreds of students and faculty. Five days later police waged a pitched battle at the IPN campus, where they killed five students, and arrested hundreds more. Claiming to have found stockpiles of weapons, the army maintained its troops at IPN though it withdrew its soldiers from UNAM.

People came and went to the demonstrations, registering their dissatisfaction with the government and their wish to have their demands for reform met. Apparently, the government, increasingly agitated about possible disruptions of the upcoming Olympics, organized a showdown on October 2 at the Plaza of the Three Cultures, the center of the wealthy section of the Nonoalco-Tlatelolco complex. On the morning of October 2, the President's special advisors took over apartments high in the Chihuahua building. Elsewhere in the same building, the Olympic Battalion, who were trained to protect people once the games began, were designated to guard the entrances to the Chihuahua building and arrest the organizers of the rally once they showed up.[26] Whatever the plan, the CNH leaders entered the building and began addressing the rally at about 6 p.m. from a third floor balcony of the Chihuahua building.

As a crowd of from 6,000 to 15,000 of students, residents, observers, and activists listened to the speeches, two helicopters flew over the complex and sent up flares. Immediately, shots sounded from the surrounding apartments, as soldiers and police snipers fired indiscriminately into the crowds in the plaza, pursuing those who scattered at the sound of gunfire. The Olympic Batallion Corp, wearing white gloves to identify themselves, invaded the Chihuahua building hoping to intercept and arrest the speakers. As the police and soldiers shot into the crowd, men and women from the neighborhood, including local housewives and members of a school football team, first counter-attacked with fists and stray objects.[27] But when the army attacked, the crowd began to run. The shooting, which lasted from about six in the afternoon to midnight resulted in forty-four deaths and a thousand or more young students and workers being wounded, imprisoned, and tortured. Hundreds more were said to have been dropped from planes in the Gulf of Mexico.[28]

According to a report published in 2006 based on intensive investigations of Mexican government and CIA files, people in the army "contravening or misintrpreting the orders of [the general in charge of the operation], utilized snipers to induce an armed response on the part of the Army. . . ." The report went on to call the event an act of "genocide" and blamed it on "a decision of the state" who, it claims, viewed the people at the rally as "an active nucleus of the national group that should be annihilated."[29] Such views underlay justifications for the massacre of Tlatelolco and tied this event to the subsequent "dirty wars" in which formally democratic governments like that of South Africa, and authoritarian governments like the military regimes in Argentina, Brazil, and Chile, simply rounded up student radicals, labor leaders, social workers, teachers, and guerrillas, held them in secret prisons, tortured them, and often murdered or "disappeared" them in the 1970s.

A different form of violence challenged democracy elsewhere in the world. While many people are afforded the luxury of thinking about democracy abstractly without knowing or even imagining what it means to fight for it on a daily basis, struggles for access to natural resources—in this case caused by floods and water scarcity—have paradoxically conferred the desire for democracy new salience. Many people attempting to secure the well-being of their families and communities according to equitable democratic principles employ the concept of "democracy" to refer to a political condition that they frequently associate with better distribution of all social, cultural, and economic and natural resources, including water, as well as with political rights of free association and free speech. Internationally, many of those determined to protect or improve the quality of life for their communities are preoccupied with their own brand of direct democracy, and one of the foremost of these groups is the Green Belt Movement of Kenya.

In the early 1970s, rural women in Kenya began realizing that their marshes, streams, and ponds that they relied on were drying up; they had to go farther and farther to collect the wood and water they needed to survive. A group of farm women contacted the National Council of Women of Kenya, a Nongovernmental Organization (NGO) made up of women's organizations from all over the country. One of the women attending the seminar was Wangari Maathai, a university professor of Veterinary Anatomy, who had grown up in rural Kenya and had attended Mount St. Scholastica College in Atchison, Kansas. The delegation of rural women attending that day explained their grievance "They didn't have enough wood for fuel or fencing, fodder for their livestock, water to cook with or drink, or enough for themselves and their families to eat.[30] The rural women, who were involved with families growing coffee for the market while they themselves farmed subsistence crops, realized that the transformations that they and their relatives had been forced to make over the previous half century, including cutting down indigenous trees to grow coffee as a cash crop, had interfered with their ability to provide healthy food for their families. The loss of domestic trees due to deforestation and the lowering of the water table forced women to travel farther each day to secure fresh water and wood. Mothers were forced to feed children more expensive processed food since it required less cooking. Some of the children began to suffer malnutrition and related diseases. For Maathai, "The connection between the symptoms of environmental degradation and their causes—deforestation, devegetation, unsustainable agriculture, and soil loss—were self-evident . . . It just came to me: Why not plant trees?"[31]

They planted the first seven saplings at a gathering in Nairobi on World Environment Day in 1977. Initially, they bought saplings from nurseries and then they began cultivating the trees themselves. The movement spread throughout Kenya, creating battalions of barefoot "foresters without diplomas." The women met together to discuss economic and social changes that had led to environmental degradation and they turned to human rights and popular democracy. Since then, the pan-African women's movement has planted billions of trees throughout Africa, launching the Pan-African Green Belt Network in

Ethiopia, Uganda, Tanzania, Malawi, Lesotho, and Zimbabwe, and creating jobs in the process.

In 1992, as political repression in Kenya increased, the government arrested large groups of young men and women who were demanding political reform and charged them with treason. Some of the Green Belt women, including Wangari Maathai, organized a hunger strike in a park in Nairobi and the police brutally attacked them with tear gas and clubs, sending many to the hospital, although they were successful in winning the release of the young people. Their struggles helped launch a decade-long movement to recreate a multiparty democracy in the country. When in 2002 Kenya held free elections, Maathai was elected to parliament and then was appointed Assistant Minister for environment and natural resources. In 2004, she won the Nobel Peace Prize.

Wangari Maathai, a professor of veterinary anatomy and a member of the National Council of Women of Kenya, consults with rural women about how best to save their land and raise the water levels by planting saplings. Explaining what drove her to fight for democracy in order to improve the environment, she said, "when you have bad governance, of course, these resources are destroyed: The forests are deforested, there is illegal logging, there is soil erosion. I got pulled deeper and deeper and saw how these issues become linked to governance, to corruption, to dictatorship." United Nations, Photo #85689

Democratic projects that include equal engagement in decision-making processes and that enable every adult to negotiate to win his or her own individual and collective aims, and such views now permeate many of the progressive social movements. Campaigns around improving the quality of life are generating new regional and transnational decentralized networks, linked by international conferences, extra-parliamentary organizations, and coordinated international demonstrations. The institutions that may grow out of such alliances are now only in an embryonic state and may not even coalesce in the near future. Nevertheless these institutions in which people engage to achieve collective well-being form the nucleus of future democratic federations around the world.

CHAPTER 8

New World Dawning

A significant result of the civil rights, student, and labor movements of the 1960s was the re-emergence in the 1970s of worldwide feminist activism, which resulted in women throughout the world demanding that their own creativity, imaginations, racial pride, and sexual concerns be incorporated into discussions about democracy. Like those women who struggled for the vote and engaged in campaigns to end slavery, exploitation, or war in the nineteenth and early twentieth centuries, late twentieth-century women in a variety of countries created vibrant democratic women's movements.

The resurgence of feminism in the 1970s and women's movements to resist or remove repressive governments in Spain, Poland, Chile, and Burma (also known as Myanmar) helped shape national and international legislation to enhance women's legal equality, education, health, and political participation and to provide individual and collective groups with influence over decision-making. Feminists organized direct democratic movements for reproductive rights, sexual freedom, and equal pay, but they also formed the mass bases for peace, environmental, and human rights campaigns.

A long-planned, clandestine feminist conference scheduled for December 1975 in Madrid occurred by chance merely three weeks after the death of dictator Francisco Franco who had ruled Spain for thirty-seven years. With authoritarian laws still in place, feminists like Lydia Falcón, who had been imprisoned because of her long struggles for human rights and women rights, met with younger feminists to formulate their goals for democratizing Spain. Many of the feminists of all classes turned their attention to repealing the adultery law that made adultery synonymous with virtually any extended contact with men to whom they were not married and defined adultery as a criminal offense punishable by the equivalent of a ten-thousand-dollar fine or six months in prison. Generally used by estranged husbands to gain custody of children (in the absence of legal divorce until 1981), the threat of a prison sentence forced many women to reluctantly give up their children. But in 1976, with the support of mass mobilizations of working-class and middle-class women in Zaragoza, Barcelona, and Madrid, nineteen women challenged the law to win their rights as sexually active women as well as mothers. Feminists, wearing signs that read "I too am an adulterer," gathered outside the courts and marched through the streets. Together they succeeded in forcing the new government to change the law as an initial step in democratizing the country.[1] Similar mobilizations occurred elsewhere to gain rights to birth control and abortions, and later to win quotas for political representation (the inclusion of women candidates on political party lists).

To some degree all of the democratic movements of the period following the First and Second World Wars incorporated women who participated in unions, political parties, and independence movements. In India between the 1920s and 1930s, activist Sarojini Naidu had helped shape the Congress Party, and, along with Mahatma Gandhi, had led mass marches of Hindu, Muslim, and Christian Indian women in opposition to the British salt tax and control of the cloth trade.[2] In the 1980s, the Self-employed Women's Association gathered Indian street vendors in locally based participant-run unions in order to defend their interests. During the Civil Rights movement in the United States, women mobilized through their local churches to provide food and care for other activists as well as to organize city-wide demonstrations that fueled the civil rights struggle. In Egypt from the 1950s on, Nawal el Saadawi and other members of the Arab Women's Solidarity Association fought against genital cutting and for women's civil and political rights.

Struggles for women's collective rights transformed politics, but feminists also campaigned to achieve individual rights. During a brief period following the triumph of the Chinese Revolution in 1949, peasant women engaged in a practice called "speaking bitterness" (*suku*) to discuss their personal struggles against family and public violence. Following their lead, 1960s feminists in the United States, Europe, and Latin America introduced their own variation called "consciousness raising," linking the personal and the political and thereby adding another dimension to efforts to democratize the household and the state. Later on, during the 1980s, feminists who were engaged in overturning the dictatorship of Augusto Pinochet in Chile demanded personal and political changes that would bring about "Democracy in the Country and in the Home." These seemingly unconnected efforts had strong repercussions on campaigns for democracy around the world.

Many of the tendencies that appeared fully formed at the end of the twentieth century had their origins thirty to fifty years earlier. For instance, in Poland, which belonged to the Soviet Bloc following the Second World War, shortages, high food prices, and excruciating work schedules led women workers such as Anna Walentynowicz to engage in the struggle for reforms. Walentynowicz had become a crane operator at the Lenin Shipyards in Gdansk in 1951. As an orphan, former indentured servant, and advocate for the rights of workers, she strongly believed in the possibilities that Communism would bring. But other workers, outraged by the increasing repression, rebelled in 1956. Although the Soviet Union purported to create workers' states—and even gave the name of "Democratic Republic" to the Eastern sector of Germany—they never promised to create workers' democracies in which the people would rule.

Without consulting any workers, the Polish government between 1966 and 1970 decided to downsize the massive shipbuilding industry in the Baltic region. With food prices already constituting half of most workers' income, the shipbuilders and the government were on a collision course in December 1970. When the government actually increased food prices on December 12, male and female workers and their families began to mobilize. On Monday, December 14, workers in Gdansk went to the shipyards but refused to work until wages were increased and food costs reduced.[3] Workers walked off the job singing both the Polish national anthem and the Communist "Internationale." They called for "democracy," though it was not clear what they meant by that word. When the army and police attacked fifteen thousand local people, killing five and injuring forty others, the workers in nearby Szczecin and Gdynia joined the strike. They demanded equalization of wages between managers and workers and the right to elect their own representatives. The government quickly retaliated, arresting the strike committee and sending in two armored divisions, leading to a sit-down strike and government occupation of the three cities where the workers were demonstrating. On Saturday, December 19, 1970, Anna Walentnyowicz and an electrician, Lech Wałęsa, organized an independent Council of Striking Workers that demanded the creation of a union free from party control.

A few months later, in February 1971, women textile workers in Łódź, though at the opposite end of the economic spectrum from the shipbuilders, also began to demand democratic changes. Not only did the women work long hours at the factory, they returned home to a "second shift," feeding and caring for their families. Low wages, high food prices, and water shortages meant that working women had to stand for hours waiting to buy water in addition to doing all of their other household chores.[4] Finding the situation intolerable, and determined to regain some control over their standard of living, eight thousand workers, primarily women, walked off the job. Their strike accomplished what the mostly male workers in the shipyards had been unable to win: the reduction of food prices back to December 12 levels. But their victory did little to increase their ultimate goal of participating in democratic management of the factories.

As in other movements to win a degree of control formerly lacking, the Polish campaign for more power over decision-making occurred over a long time in a variety of incidents. First, there were further protests against increased food costs in June 1976. Then the KOR (the Workers' Defense Committee), formed in September 1976, brought students, white-color workers, journalists, and other intellectuals into coalition with the workers. In May 1977, Anna Walentnyowicz found out about KOR in church and over Radio Free Europe, broadcast by the United States. Almost two years later, Walentnyowicz was arrested for her role in the annual event commemorating the workers killed in December 1970. Although the government seems to have tried to turn her into an informer and then charged her with theft, she regained her job when her fellow workers struck back in her defense. And at the level of access to international media, nothing was more important for the Polish workers' movement than the October 1978 elevation of Cardinal Karol Wojtyla, archbishop of Crakow, to the position of Pope John Paul II.

But that alone would not have enhanced the break with the previous regime had it not been for the success of Solidarity, the union formed in 1980. Despite the militant resistance, even moderate demands for democracy can take decades as was the case with the struggle for independent unions in Poland. When the Polish government again raised food prices in July 1980, and fired Walentynowicz on August 7 after twenty-eight years on the job and just five months short of her retirement, the ship workers' union gathered and decided to strike on August 14. Early in the morning, 8,000 out of the 17,000 workers, including Walentynowicz, forced the head of the Lenin Shipyard to speak to them over loudspeakers so that everyone occupying the shipyards could hear the negotiations.[5]

Thirty-five independent organizations formed and demanded increased wages, improved food supplies, and widespread publication of the strikers' demands, and called on the government to recognize them as a single, self-governing trade union they called "Solidarity."[6] Defying all odds, the Polish workers won recognition of their union on November 1980, but that was not the end of the story (see Figure 8.1).

In 1981, the threat of a Soviet invasion allegedly led Prime Minister General Wojciech Jaruzelski to declare martial law and arrest many of Solidarity's leaders. The Nobel Prize Committee's award of the Peace Prize to Lech Wałęsa in October 1983, and the accession to power of reformer Mikhail Gorbachev as the general secretary of the Communist Party of the Soviet Union in March 1985, helped Solidarity win an amnesty for all the political prisoners in September 1986. Three years later, on April 17, 1989, Solidarity gained legal recognition as an independent, self-governing trade union. A political coalition,

A member of the independent labor movement Solidarity photographed fellow members including Anna Walentynowicz, one of the union's founders, attending one of the Masses for the Homeland in Saint Stanislav Kostka Church in Warsaw, led by priest Jerzy Popieluszko, in 1983. Until Father Jerzy Popieluszko's 1984 assassination by Poland's secret police, he held regular masses in support of Solidarity, at which parishioners held up a "V" for victory against state repression. Photo by Andzej Iwański with Communists in the minority, formed in September 1988, and, in February 1989, Poland was once again declared a democratic republic.

During roughly the same period, countries like Chile moved in the opposite direction, away from democracy. Before the military coup of September 11, 1973, Chile was regarded as one of the most democratic countries in Latin America. According to popular opinion a bicameral legislature, frequent elections, and strong municipal governmental bodies assured Chile a place in the congress of democratic nations.

In 1970, Chileans elected Salvador Allende, the first socialist elected president of any country in the Americas. His overthrow in a military coup greatly assisted by the United States challenged Chileans more than most other people to think about how they would define democracy and how far they were willing to go to reinstate it.

Allende, a doctor by profession, had run for president and been defeated in 1952, 1958, and 1964. But with only a plurality of 36.6 percent of the vote, he finally came to power at the head of a coalition government called the Popular Unity (Unidad Popular) that was dedicated to loosening the constraints on democracy. A coalition of wealthy landowners, supporters of those in collusion with foreign copper mining interests and telegraph companies immediately attempted to persuade the army to intervene and oust the newly elected government. A foreign embargo on sending supplies to Chile assured that food and other supplies would sharply diminish. The Popular Unity government attempted to build houses, provide food, especially milk to children, liberalize landholding, and improve education throughout the country. The United States, through the Central Intelligence Agency (CIA), had poured money into radio broadcasts, through which the great majority of Chileans, especially women, got most of their information.

Once Allende won the election, the United States, in the words of President Richard M. Nixon, vowed to "squeeze the economy [of Chile] until it screamed."[7] When food shortages ensued, the Minister of Economy, Development, and Reconstruction called a "town meeting" in one of the largest soccer stadiums in Chile to discuss what was causing supplies to decline and prices to rise. He explained to an audience primarily of women what the government intended to do about improving the economy, and invited the women's comments and suggestions about how to improve conditions.[8] But nothing further was done to elicit ideas from ordinary people.

The government's nationalization of the copper mines and paper mills led many on the right to assume that Allende was moving toward a Soviet—or at least Cuban—style government. The right-wing argued that the nationalization of paper was the first step toward ending free-dom of the press by preventing conservative newspapers from publishing their views. Women from the right-wing parties raised fears that educational reform, designed to provide places in school for millions of children previously excluded from an education, was part of a plot to turn children, Nazi style, into spies against their parents. The shortages, strikes, and rising prices from June to September 1973 led to mass mobilizations of people on all sides. The army chief of staff who defended Allende's attempts to hold the country together was humiliated and forced to resign, leading Allende to appoint a previously loyal general, Augusto Pinochet, as chief of staff. On September 11, 1973, as the air force bombed the presidential palace, Allende delivered his final speech over the radio. Explaining that he would certainly "pay for the loyalty of the people with [his] life" he claimed "that the seed which we have planted in the good conscience of thousands and thousands of Chileans [would] not be shriveled forever" because "other men [would] overcome this dark and bitter moment when treason seeks to prevail." He urged his fellow citizens to "go forward knowing that, sooner rather than later, the great avenues will open again where free men will walk to build a better society."[9]

The coup, according to the 1975 report, "Covert Action in Chile, 1963–1973," issued by the Senate Select Committee to Study Governmental Operations with Respect to Intelligence Activities, provided strong evidence of the complicity of the CIA in the overthrow of Salvador Allende. Opponents of the military dictatorship led by Pinochet, and even those who had merely worked among the poor were rounded up, tortured in soccer stadiums, army camps, aboard navy ships, and in former political centers, and frequently murdered. As men and women, particularly workers, doctors, nurses, school teachers, and college students, began to disappear, many of their fathers and mothers set out to look for and find their disappeared children.

Parents and friends formed the Association of the Families of the Disappeared and began carrying signs bearing their children's pictures. Some of the impoverished mothers gathered in workshops organized by the Catholic Church to prepare burlap tapestries for sale. These handiworks called *arpilleras* played the role of a free press and illustrated abductions, food kitchens, and demonstrations such as one that extraordinarily brave women staged by chaining themselves to the gates of Congress that the military had closed down.

The repression was so great during the first ten years of the dictatorship that, apart from dangerous commemorations of International

Women's Day on March 8, 1978, and 1979, there were few public mobilizations. But soon, the families whose loved ones had been murdered or disappeared were joined in the early 1980s by liberal political party activists and feminists, who called for the return to democracy. Their prime avenue of expression was through political demonstrations of which the feminist gathering outside the National Library in downtown Santiago was the most stirring. Carrying a banner calling for "Democracy Now [the] Feminist Movement [of] Chile", feminists led by Julieta Kirkwood linked the issues of the emancipation of women as full citizens to the need for the democratization of the entire country.

When the father of two murdered college students set himself on fire in 1982, groups from all of the liberal and leftist clandestine parties began to take action. Women from a variety of underground parties called a mass meeting between Christmas and New Year's, and thousands of women showed up, though all public meetings were still prohibited. These women, a coalition of various groups united only by

Julieta Kirkwood and other Chilean feminists risked their lives to challenge the decade-long dictatorship of Augusto Pinochet by gathering at the public library in downtown Santiago on August 11, 1983. Holding a sign saying "Democracy Now, the Feminist Movement of Chile," they were among the leaders of the opposition movement that ultimately succeeded in restoring democracy to Chile in 1988. Photo by Kena Lorenzini

their wish for the return of democracy, began to call themselves *Mujeres por la Vida*, Women for Life, to mitigate the politics of death that had separated Chile from its democratic institutions. Political activists began to organize clandestinely, hoping to formulate new democratic platforms from which they could negotiate a return to democracy. Differences among them reduced their power, but they could agree at first on the need for mass mobilizations. These began in 1982 and continued through 1988, when opposition groups, including *Mujeres por la Vida*, mobilized to defeat Pinochet, whose tailor-made constitution provided for his "election" in 1988 for an additional eight-year-term as president. With mock balloting, inviting motorists and pedestrians to vote out the dictatorship, and through television spot announcements, *Mujeres por la Vida* and the dissident political parties called for a repudiation of Pinochet through a "no" vote in the coming plebiscite that was to determine whether he should continue ruling Chile. To the surprise of the dictatorship, which continued to impede dissent through widespread arrests, the "no" vote won, and the dissident parties and the government negotiated free elections. Although Pinochet was made a Senator for Life, Chile was able to re-establish a parliamentary democracy in 1991.

The new government of Chile established an investigative body to discover how many people had been killed and how many had disappeared during the authoritarian regime. The Rettig Committee, as Chile's investigative body was called, documented 3,065 deaths, though subsequent committees have raised the total number of certified instances of torture and death to 40,000.

In addition to the use of government commissions to investigate past national abuses, certain countries began using United Nations' human rights legislation to enforce people's democratic rights wherever torture had occurred. In a landmark case in October 1998, Balthazar Garzón, a Spanish prosecutorial judge, charged Augusto Pinochet for violations of international human rights laws. Great Britain's Scotland Yard charged Pinochet and held him under house arrest for fifteen months until the House of Lords—Britain's supreme court—ruled that Pinochet was suffering from dementia, could not adequately defend himself, and therefore could not stand trial. But the process highlighted the willingness of international bodies to offer legal protections of human rights and, by extension, democratic rights beyond national borders.

Most progressive revolutions promise widespread future benefits, but how do hopes for democracy or commitment to achieving it stay alive or get reborn after year upon year of repression? The Tiananmen Square Uprising in 1989 highlights the power of democratic aspirations despite the persistence of continued disappointments. During the wars against the Japanese and the Nationalist Party in the 1930s and 1940s, Chinese women farmers formed democratic governing councils called *soviets*. And male and female peasants belonged to large peasant and women's leagues, which, though run from above, also permitted some degree of democratic participation at the local level. But these associations were dissolved once the revolution succeeded in 1949. During China's Great Leap Forward from 1958 to 1961, the country underwent massive industrialization with no democratic participation in decision-making. Then the Cultural Revolution from 1966 to 1976, when age and custom themselves came under attack, virtually precluded democratic organizing of any kind. Yet by 1978, two years after the Cultural Revolution ended, groups of youthful students, eager to open up a discussion of democratic reforms, hung posters on a wall called "the Triangle" at Beijing University and elsewhere. The poster movement quickly became known as the Democracy Wall Movement, and Wei Jingsheng, whom the government targeted as the leader of this movement, was condemned to fourteen years in prison.[10]

In 1989, after a period of unrest among urban college graduates, China approached the seventieth anniversary of the May 4th movement and the fortieth anniversary of the triumph of the Communist Revolution. As the government introduced a market economy causing prices to fluctuate and any trust in the evenhandedness of the government declined, there were rumblings throughout the country. The death on April 15, 1989, of Hu Yaobang, former secretary general of the Communist Party, set off a flurry of student demonstrations in Beijing and other large Chinese cities. He was believed to have been demoted in 1987 after five years in office because of his opposition to the repression of human rights activists. In Beijing, between April 16 and April 21, 1989, increasing numbers of students gathered at Tiananmen Square to honor Hu and to call for a free press, freedom of assembly, and the right to meet with government leaders for open discussions. The newly formed Autonomous Federation of Students coordinated activities throughout the city and planned to ally with students elsewhere in the country. On May Day, students in Shanghai called for a demonstration the next day to demand a free press, the right to demonstrate, and freedom to organize.[11] In fifty-one cities, students and other citizens followed their lead and called for "democracy, science, freedom, human rights, and rule by law."[12]

The Eight Institutes of Art in Beijing brought a statue of the Goddess of Democracy into Tiananmen Square in 1989, placing her directly opposite the large photograph of Mao Zedong. The declaration the art students distributed explained, "Our great and dignified Chinese people have finally broken through autocracy and forged an upsurge of democracy. . . . Today on the square of the people stands the statue of the people's Goddess of Democracy. She declares to the world that the great awakening of the Chinese people to democratic ideas has reached a new stage. The trees of democracy and freedom are being planted in this ancient land, and they will blossom most splendidly and bear the richest fruit." AP Photo/Jeff Widener

On May 4, 1989 thousands of people gathered in the square. In a gesture of self-abnegation, about 300 students began a hunger strike on May 13 to persuade the government to enter into dialogue, and the number of hunger strikers quickly grew to 3,000. Then the student movement spread, and by May 17, an estimated one million people from all walks of life filled the square in defense of democratic change.[13] When the government decided to crack down and ordered one hundred thousand soldiers to put an end to the hunger strikers' demonstration, over two million people blocked their way. More and more people acting as citizens poured into the streets. On May 29, students from the Central Academy of Fine Arts entered the square wheeling in their Goddess of Democracy, modeled on the Statue of Liberty of the United States.[14] The government declared martial law, and, on the night of June 3 and the morning of June 4, the army cleared Tiananmen Square, killing more than a thousand people in the process. Although other thousands have been arrested since then, the movement for democracy has remained alive as countless groups of dissidents have stepped forward with democratic claims.

A minor controversy over whether the grass-roots nongovernmental portion of the Fourth United Nations World Conference on Women, scheduled for late August and early September 1995, should take place in Beijing or forty miles away in the village of Hairou brought to the fore questions about the multiple venues of democracy. The Chinese authorities, fearing mass mobilizations in Beijing, relegated the nongovernmental portion of the conference to Hairou. Yet, as in previous United Nations' women's conferences, like the 1975 World Conference of the International Women's Year held in Mexico City, activists used the opportunity to importune official delegates and capture the attention of the world press to make their case for democracy.

One universally acclaimed woman at the portion of the conference in Beijing was Aung San Suu Kyi, the winner of the 1991 Nobel Peace Prize. Long hailed by human rights activists as a new Gandhi or Nelson Mandela, Aung San Suu Kyi fulfilled the role of the selfless human rights advocate and the leader of democratic aspirations in Burma.[15] Her father, Aung San, like many other successful leaders of anti-imperialist struggles following the Second World War, was assassinated a few years after he helped carry out the successful transition to independence. Aung San Suu Kyi, born in 1942, became the dutiful daughter caring for her widowed mother, who served as the ambassador to India in 1960. A member of the Burmese elite, Aung San Suu Kyi was well educated in the colleges and universities of Burma, India, and the United Kingdom. Following her studies at Oxford, Suu Kyi married Michael Aris, a British scholar of Tibetan literature. Moving among Bhutan, the United States, and the United Kingdom, the couple had two sons. Suu Kyi worked in the Bodleian Library in Oxford and wrote a biography of her father. The young family traveled and taught and finally settled in the United Kingdom until Suu Kyi's mother's stroke in 1988 brought her back to Burma, where she remained until liberalization and free elections occurred in the spring of 2012.

From 1962 through the first decade of the twenty-first century, military dictators and their supporters waged continuous battles against the forces of democracy in Burma. Suu Kyi's return coincided with a massive uprising known as the "Four Eights"—since it erupted on August 8, 1988—that resulted in the death of over ten thousand people fighting for what they called democracy. Suu Kyi did not initiate

Demonstrators in Burma called for the removal of two articles from the 2008 constitution explicitly directed against Aung San Suu Kyi of the National League for Democracy. Article 59d insisted that all candidates for president must belong to the military or have expertise in economic and political matters, and Article 59f precluded anyone whose spouse or children were citizens of another nation, as Aung San Suu Kyi's late husband was and two sons are.
AP photo/Jeff Widener

this movement, but she quickly joined it and soon became its figure-head. Promising democratic changes, a right-wing junta, calling itself the State Law and Order Restoration Council, nevertheless imposed even more repressive laws when it took power in mid-September 1988. Shortly thereafter, Aung San Suu Kyi and her ally U Tin Oo formed the National League for Democracy as a coordinating body for the legion of local organizations fighting to win rights of free speech, assembly, publication, and elections. Between 1988 and 2002, Suu Kyi was held under house arrest. In and out of isolation, Suu Kyi served as a sym-bol of hope for free elections and an end to military government. Her organization established a presence so that even when banned, as in the elections of May 1990, they won huge support. Imprisoned at home again in 2000, she was released in 2002 with the promise that she would not call for the overthrow of the military government while pro-moting democratic change. A surprising thaw under the guidance of President Thein Sein led her and her party to participate in what they believed would finally be free elections, where they won forty-three of the forty-five Parliamentary seats in contention, one of which went to Aung San Suu Kyi.[16]

The so-called Burmese Spring that achieved free elections took its name from the Arab Spring. The Arab Spring began more than a year earlier with the self-immolation of a harassed and exploited Tunisian fruit vendor in December 2010 and subsequently turned into an eighteen-day uprising in February 2011 that toppled the nearly thirty-year-long army rule of Hosni Mubarak in Egypt. The President of Tunisia was driven out in mid-January, the President of Yemen in June, and Muammar Gaddafi fell and was killed in October 2011 after a NATO-supported rebellion in Libya.

Although many of these movements were responses to widespread repression, inequalities, and the absence of the possibilities for advance-ment of the most highly educated sectors of the population, they all promoted hope for the creation of new democratic societies. Like demo-cratic movements that had emerged in 1848, these new uprisings simply wanted to remove repressive authorities and put a more diverse group of people in power. In fact, Janos Kovacs, a Hungarian dissident in the 1980s, may have expressed the views of 1848 and 2011 to 2012 most clearly when he was asked how he became a proponent of democracy. He cryptically responded that he had seen a lot of American movies that took place in junior high school. Asked to clarify what he meant, he explained that you do not need a well-developed political program to realize that there has to be something better than that.[17] Most of the democratic movements that followed the Arab Spring in Egypt, Tunisia, Spain, Greece, the United States, Chile, and Canada—to name just a few—demanded increased popular participation in governing their countries or changes in neoliberal economic policies that sought to reduce government spending in the public sector. In many of these countries, cuts in the pensions of public workers, privatization of public schools and universities, mortgage foreclosures as workers in all sectors were laid off, and increased dependency of adult children on the pensions of aged family members marked disastrous changes for a large portion of the population.

Initially, as in Egypt, the chief protagonists of the uprisings seemed to be young people fueled by outrage over political repression and the absence of jobs. Equipped with the technology of social media, they expanded their venues and reached out beyond local and national borders to attack repressive governments and corruption. By placing the needs of the many above the profits of a few, and by creating direct democratic practices, all of the self-proclaimed democratic movements hoped to transform their societies in more egalitarian directions. But, unlike late nineteenth- and early twentieth-century uprisings, the early twenty-first century movements refused to promote any specific party or concentrate their energy on advancing one specific political strategy over another. Instead of working in local, regional, or national elections, they mostly participated in popular assemblies or factory seizures in which strategies and goals were worked out in public and implemented through direct action rather than through any representative political institutions.[18] Many of their movements have been crushed. Some have succeeded to a lesser degree and in different ways than they had hoped. Many find themselves continuing to fight for rights they thought they had won in the past. And yet, the mobilizations, assemblies, and efforts to coordinate demonstrations across states and nations in the name of democracy indicated, to the optimistic, the idea that eternal springs might some day lead to new awakenings and renewed possibilities for democracy.

Chronology

1750 BCE
Creation of the Hammurabi Code, the oldest known complete legal system

7TH–4TH CENTURIES BCE
Direct and participatory democracy flourishes throughout the Greek city-state of Athens

100–800 AD
The agricultural civilization of the Moche people in Perú creates autonomous and self-governed polities based on mutual cooperation and interdependence around water

1155
The Cortes of León meets for the first time

1215
Known as an early precursor to the rule of constitutional law, the Magna Carta is imposed upon the King of England in an attempt to limit his powers and protect the rights of feudal barons

1520–21
The communero revolt pits the cities of Castile against Charles V over taxation and urban rights

1653
The Dutch arrive in South Africa, initiating what would become three centuries of Afrikaner and British subjugation of Africans and Indian immigrants

JULY 3, 1776
Declaration of Independence signed, launching the American Revolution

1781–1804
A slave Revolution results in the Haitian war of independence. In 1804 the

French are defeated, all slaves are freed, and the victors form the Republic of Haiti

JULY 14, 1789
Start of the French Revolution raises questions of nationalism and seeks to expand human rights throughout France

1848
British Chartists attempt to win universal male suffrage, but are defeated; the Taiping Rebellion leads to social changes for millions of women as well as men under the rule of the Heavenly Kingdom; democratic revolutions break out all over Europe and its colonies. Elizabeth Cady Stanton writes the "Declaration of Sentiments," a declaration of independence for women as citizens

1893
In New Zealand, the first group of women in history gain full suffrage rights.

1910–20
Emiliano Zapata and his soldiers from Morelos join the many groups fighting in the Mexican Revolution and claim their rights to land and freedom

1917
The February and October Revolutions succeed in overthowing the tsar of Russia and set the stage for other world revolutions. Mexico passes what is considered to be the first modern constitution by addressing social as well as political rights

1944
The Serviceman's Readjustment Act, also known as the G.I. Bill, is passed in the United States expanding access to

education and training to a generation of veterans returning from the Second World War.

NOVEMBER 20, 1945–OCTOBER 1, 1946
The Nuremburg Trials indict and convict several Nazis perpetrators of the Holocaust for "crimes against humanity"

OCTOBER 24, 1946
In the aftermath of the Second World War, the United Nations is established to promote cooperation among nations using a democratic framework among member states

JUNE 3, 1947
After decades of struggle and a successful nonviolent campaign of civil-disobedience led by Mahatma Ghandi, India wins its independence from Britain

1952 TO 1956
Defiance Campaign that first challenged Apartheid through mass action took place in South Africa between 1952 and 1953; Montgomery Bus Boycott began in Montgomery, Alabama, launched by Rosa Parks in December 1955 and led by Martin Luther King Jr. and the Montgomery Improvement Association

JANUARY 1, 1959
Cuban rebels succeed in overthrowing the repressive dictatorship of Fulgencio Batista with the aim of expanding rights for the Cuban people

1968
Revolutions led by students and workers sweep Europe and the Americas from Czechoslovakia and Poland to France and Mexico calling for democratic changes and an end to militarism

DECEMBER 19, 1970
Lech Wałęsa and Anna Walentnyowicz launch the Council of Striking Workers that demands the creation of a union free from party control in Poland

SEPTEMBER 11, 1973
Salvador Allende's democratically elected socialist government in Chile is overthrown in a military coup, with help from the CIA

1977
Wangari Maathai starts the Green Belt Movement in Kenya, organizing women throughout Africa to combat deforestation and soil erosion through nonviolent participatory democracy

FEBRUARY 1989
Poland is declared a democratic republic after Solidarity gains legal recognition as a self-governing trade union and joins a coalition to govern the country

JUNE 3, 1989
The Chinese government attacks and kills over a thousand protestors demanding democratic reforms at Tiananmen Square

APRIL 27, 1994
Nelson Mandela is sworn in as President of South Africa culminating eighty-two years of struggle by the ANC and starting a transition away from Apartheid into majority rule and the creation of a more inclusive constitution and society

2012
Aung San Suu Kyi is elected to Parliament in Burma, after decades of struggle for democratic change

Notes

INTRODUCTION

1. Sir Winston Churchill, Speech in the House of Commons, November 11, 1947, Hansard. Verbatim transcripts of Parliamentary Debates in Britain. Hansard Archive (digitized debates from 1803), www.parliament.uk; http://www.publications.parliament.uk/pa/cm200708/cmhansard/cm071122/haltext/1122h0002.htm (pt0002).

CHAPTER 1

1. The Code of Hammurabi, translated by L. W. King, http://www.general-intelligence.com/library/hr.pdf.
2. The Code of Hammurabi, translated by L. W. King, http://www.general-intelligence.com/library/hr.pdf.
3. Luís Jaime Castillo Butters, "Moche Politics in the Jequetepeque Valley: A Case for Political Opportunism," in *New Perspectives on Moche Political Organization*, ed. Jeffrey Quilter and Luis Jaime Castillo B. (Washington, DC: Dumbarton Oaks Research Library and Collection, 2010), 83, 88, 104, and 109n1.
4. Barbara Fash, William Fash, Sheree Lane, Rudy Larios, Linda Schele, Jeffrey Stomper and David Stuart, "Investigations of a Classic Maya Council House at Copán, Honduras," *Journal of Field Archaeology, 19*, no.4 (1992): 419-442.
5. Fekri A. Hassan, "The Dynamics of a Riverine Civilization: A Geological Perspective on the Nile Valley, Egypt," *World Archeology* 29, no.1 (1997): 51–74; at 55, 56, 69.
6. Sandra Postel, *Pillar of Sand: Can the Irrigation Miracle Last?* (New York: W. W. Norton, 1999).
7. Lionel Casson, *Everyday Life in Ancient Egypt*, 2nd ed. (Baltimore: Johns Hopkins Press, 2001), 36–37.
8. Donald Kagan, *Pericles of Athens and the Birth of Democracy* (New York: Free Press, 1991), 138.
9. Solon Biography at http://www.PoemHunter.com; see also Life of Solon, by Plutarch About.com, http://ancienthistory.about.com/library/bl/bl_text_plutarch_solon.htm.
10. Kagan, *Pericles of Athens and the Birth of Democracy*, 15.
11. M. I. Finley, *The Ancient Greeks* (1963; repr., New York: Penguin Books, 1991), 30.
12. Pericles, "In Defense of Democracy," cited by Thucydides in *The Peloponnesian War*, http://www.cooperativeindividualism.org/pericles_in-defense-of-democracy.html.
13. Plutarch, "Tiberius Gracchus," p. 3, translated by John Dryden, written in 75 CE, http://classics.mit.edu/Plutarch/tiberius.html.

14. Robin Lane Fox, *The Classical World: An Epic History from Homer to Hadrian* (New York: Perseus, 2002), 335.

15. Ibid., 335–36.

16. Steven Ozment, *The Age of Reform 1250-1550: An Intellectual and Religious History of Late Medieval and Reformation Europe* (New Haven: Yale University Press, 1980), 139.

17. Patricia Crone, *God's Rule: Government and Islam* (New York: Columbia University Press, 2004), 66–69.

18. Ozment, *The Age of Reform*, 144.

19. "The Magna Carta" (The Great Charter), http://www.constitution.org/eng/magnacar.htm.

20. John Hudson, "Magna Carta. The *ius commune*, and English Common Law," in *Magna Carta and the England of King John*, ed. Janet S. Loengard (Woodbridge, UK: Boydell Press, 2010), 99–119, at 106.

CHAPTER 2

1. For material on Gurū Nānak and the Sikhs, see J. S. Grewal, *The Sikhs: Ideology, Institutions, and Identity* (New Delhi: Oxford University Press, 2009); W. H. McLeod, *Sikhs and Sikhism: Gurū Nānak and the Sikh Religion. Early Sikh Tradition. The Evolution of the Sikh Community. Who Is a Sikh?* (New Delhi: Oxford University Press, 1999); Kharak Singh, *Guru Nanak: A Prophet with a Difference* (Amitsar: Guru Nanak Dev University, 2007).

2. Singh, *Guru Nanak*, 37–93.

3. Quoted in Singh, *Guru Nanak*, 136.

4. Aurelio Espinosa, *The Empire of the Cities: Emperor Charles V, the Comunero Revolt, and the Transformation of the Spanish System* (Leiden and Boston: Brill, 2009), 61–62.

5. Alonso de Santa Cruz, cited in Henry Latimer Seaver, *The Great Revolt in Castile: A Study of the Comunero Movement of 1520-21* (1928; repr., New York: Octagon Books, 1966), 222.

6. The formative work on the role of John Lilburne and the Levellers is Christopher Hill, *The World Turned Upside Down: Radical Ideas during the English Revolution* (1972; repr., New York and Harmondsworth, Middlesex, England: Penguin Books, 1982).

7. Hilary Mantel's *Wolf Hall* provides powerful insights into the religious and political world of King Henry VIII. See Mantel, *Wolf Hall* (New York: Henry Holt and Company, 2009).

8. John Lilburne, William Walwyn, Thomas Prince, Richard Overton, "An Agreement of the Free People of England. Tendered as a Peace-Offering to this distressed Nation." May 1, 1649, http://www.constitution.org/eng/agreepeo.htm.

9. Ann Hughes, "Lilburne, Elizabeth," *Oxford Dictionary of National Biography*, http://www.oxforddnb.com/view/article/67256.

10. Cited in J. P. S. Uberoi, *Religion, Civil Society and the State: A Study of Sikhism* (Delhi: Oxford University Press, 1999), 69–70.

CHAPTER 3

1. There is a rich bibliography on Paul Revere. For a sampling, please consult David Hackett Fischer, *Paul Revere's Ride* (New York and Oxford: Oxford University Press, 1994); Esther Forbes, *Paul Revere & The World He Lived In* (1942; repr., New York: Mariner Books, Houghton-Mifflin Harcourt, 1999); and Jayne

E. Triber, *A True Republican: The Life of Paul Revere* (Amherst, MA: University of Massachusetts Press, 1998).

2. Stamp Act Congress—1765. In Congress in New York (October 1765), http://www.ushistory.org/declaration/related/sac65.htm.

3. Joan Wallach Scott, *Only Paradoxes to Offer: French Feminists and the Rights of Man* (Cambridge, MA: Harvard University Press, 1996), 30.

4. Darline Gay Levy, Harriet Branson Applewhite, and Mary Durham Johnson, *Women in Revolutionary Paris, 1789-95* (Urbana, IL: University of Illinois Press, 1979), 90.

5. Dominique Godineau, *The Women of Paris and Their French Revolution* (1988), trans. Katherine Streip (Berkeley: University of California Press, 1998), 102–4.

6. Ibid., 105–7.

7. Ibid., 200.

8. Dauril Alden, *"Late Colonial Brazil, 1750-1808," in Colonial Brazil*, ed. Leslie Bethell (Cambridge: Cambridge University Press, 1987), 337.

9. Kenneth Maxwell, *Conflicts and Conspiracies: Brazil and Portugal, 1750-1808* (New York and London: Routledge, 2004), 139.

10. Alden, "Late Colonial Brazil," 339.

11. Ernesto Páramo, Nancy Harb Almendras, and Fausto Guidice, "Bahia, Brazil, 1798: The Revolution of the Black Jacobins," Tlaxcala, The Translators' Network for Linguistic Diversity, http://www.tlaxcala.es/pp.asp?lg=en&reference=4655.

12. [12] A.J.R. Russell-Wood, *The Black Man in Slavery and Freedom in Colonial Brazil* (London: Macmillan in association with St. Anthony's College, Oxford, 1982), 135-160; Elizabeth W. Kiddy, *Blacks of the Rosary: Memory and History in Minas Gerais, Brazil* (University Park, PA: Pennsylvania State University Press, 2005), 16, 22.

13. James Madison, "The Federalist No. 10, The Utility of the Union as a Safeguard Against Domestic Faction and Insurrection (continued)," November 22, 1787, http://www.constitution.org/fed/federa10.htm.

14. James Madison, "The Federalist No. 48, These Departments Should Not Be So Far Separated as to Have No Constitutional Control Over Each Other," February 1, 1788, http://www.constitution.org/fed/federa48.htm.

CHAPTER 4

1. Napoleon Bonaparte, "Proclamation to the French Troops in Italy (April 26, 1796)," http://www.historyguide.org/intellect/nap1796.html.

2. Wayne Hanley, *The Genesis of Napoleonic Propaganda* (1796–99), Project Gutenburg, 2002), 14, http://www.gutenberg-e.org/haw01/haw03.html.

3. Napoleon Bonaparte, "Proclamation to the French Troops in Italy (April 26, 1796)," http://www.historyguide.org/intellect/nap1796.html.

4. Velentin Boulan, "How Important Was Napoleon Bonaparte's Use of Propaganda and Censorship in the Rise and Consolidation of His Power in France," http://publishistory.wordpress.com/tag/france

5. Napoleon Bonaparte, "Proclamation to the French Troops in Italy (April 26, 1796)," http://www.historyguide.org/intellect/nap1796.html.

6. Ted Vincent, "The Blacks Who Freed Mexico," *The Journal of Negro History* 79, no. 3 (Summer 1994): 257–76, at 259.

7. P. V. Ranade, "Genetics of Russian Revolutionary Vision, 1825-1917," *Indian Journal of Political Science* 41, no.4 (December 1980): 543–85.

8. Nikita M. Murav'ev's draft Constitution, in Marc Raeff, *The Decemberist Movement* (Englewood Cliffs, NJ: Prentice Hall, Inc., 1966), 101–2.

9. Ranade, "Genetics of Russian Revolutionary Vision, 1825-1917," 556–63.

10. Malcolm Chase, *Chartism: A New History* (Manchester: University of Manchester Press, 2007), 8–9.

11. Priscilla Robertson, *Revolutions of 1848: A Social History* (Princeton: Princeton University Press, 1952), 232.

12. Ibid., 62.

13. Robert Goldstein, "Civil Liberties and the 1848 Revolutions," in *Encyclopedia of Revolutions of 1848*, ed.and trans. James G. Chastain (1998; 2005), http://www.ohio.edu/chastain/contents.htm.

14. Robertson, *Revolutions of 1848*, 206–30; Rolf Weber, "March Revolution," in *Encyclopedia of Revolutions of 1848*, http://www.ohio.edu/chastain/contents.htm.

15. "13th Amendment to the U.S. Constitution: Abolition of Slavery (1865)," http://www.ourdocuments.gov/doc.php?flash=true&doc-40.

16. The section on Seneca Falls is highly dependent on Vivian Gornick, *The Solitude of Self: Thinking About Elizabeth Cady Stanton*, (New York: Farrar, Straus, and Giroux, 2005) and on a series of anonymous articles that appeared on historynet that can be consulted at http://www.historynet.com/seneca-fallsconvention, p. 4.

17. Gornick, 39-40; and "Report of the Woman's Rights Convention: Seneca Falls, N.Y., July 19-20, 1848," in *Women's Rights Emerges within the Antislavery Movement 1830-1870: A Brief History with Documents*, ed. Kathryn Kish Sklar (New York: Bedford/St. Martins, 2000), 170–72.

18. http://www.historynet.com/seneca-fallsconvention, p.5.

19. Ibid.

20. Elizabeth Cady Stanton, *The National Reformer* (September 14, 1848), reproduced in *History of Women's Suffrage*: 1848-1861, (eds) Elizabeth Cady Stanton, Susan Brownell Anthony, and Matilda Joslyn Gage (New York: Fowler and Wells, 1881), 806. Books.google.com/books?id=6R1BAAAAYAAJ

21. S. Y. Teng, *The Taiping Rebellion and the Western Powers: A Comprehensive Survey* (Oxford: The Clarendon Press, 1971), 19; and Vincent Y. C. Shih, *The Taiping Ideology: Its Sources, Interpretations, and Influences* (Seattle: University of Washington Press, 1967), 305 and 308.

22. Franz H. Michael, in collaboration with Chung-li Chang *The Taiping Rebellion: History and Documents*, trans. Margery Anneberg et al., 3 vols. (Seattle: University of Washington Press, 1966), 1:12–13.

23. Ibid., 25, 27–28.

24. Delia Davin, *Woman-Work: Women and the Party in Revolutionary China* (Oxford: The Clarendon Press, 1976), 7.

25. Michael, 59; Shih, 300; for a less favorable assessment of what the Taiping offered women, see Denise Gimpel, "Taiping Rebellion," in *The Oxford Encyclopedia of Women in World History*, ed. Bonnie G. Smith (New York: Oxford University Press, 2008), 4:193–94.

26. Ibid., 147, 196–197.

27. Teng, 154–55.

28. Ibid., 167–68, and 174

29. Louisa Lawson, speech to the inaugural meeting of the Dawn Club. Published in *Dawn* (July 1889), http://www.abc.net.au/ola/citizen/women/women-home-vote.htm.

30. "Maceo's Letter to President Estrada Palma" (May 16, 1876), http://www.historyofcuba.com/history/maceoltr1.htm.

31. Tulia Falleti, "Antonio Maceo: The Bronze Titan," *A Political Atlas of the African Diaspora, 1900-1989* (The Institute for Diaspora

Studies, Northwestern University), citing Antonio Maceo from Philip S. Foner, *Antonio Maceo. The "Bronze Titan" of Cuba's Struggle for Independence* (New York: Monthly Review Press, 1977), 81–82, http://diaspora.northwestern.edu/mbin/WebObjects/DiasporaX.woa/wa/displayArticle?atomid=422.

32. Ada Ferrer, *Insurgent Cuba: Race, Nation and Revolution, 1868-1898* (Chapel Hill: University of North Carolina Press, 1999), 160–67.

CHAPTER 5

1. Anna Macias, "Women and the Mexican Revolution, 1910-1920," *The Americas* 36, no. 1 (July 1980): 53–82, at 60.

2. Outstanding considerations of Emilio Zapata's relation to the Mexican Revolution can be found in John Womack Jr.'s *Zapata and the Mexican Revolution* (New York: Vintage Books, 1968) and Samuel Brunk's *Emilio Zapata, Revolutionary Betrayal in Mexico* (Albuquerque: University of New Mexico Press, 1995), 12–13.

3. Brunk, 18, 27–28.

4. Macías, 58–61.

5. Ibid., 67; "Plan of Ayala" in *The Mexico Reader: History, Culture, Politics* ed. Gilbert M. Joseph and Timothy J. Henderson (Durham and London: Duke University Press, 2002), 342.

6. Mexican Constitution, Article 123, title 6.

7. Dorothy Page, *The Suffragists: Women Worked for the Vote. Essays from the Dictionary of New Zealand Biography* (Wellington, New Zealand: Bridget Williams Books/Department of Internal Affairs, 1993), http://www.nzhistoryet.nz/files/documents/womenandthevoteinNewZealand.pdf.

8. Leon Trotsky, "Chapter 8, The Creation of the Soviet of Workers' Deputies," http://www.marxist.org/archive History/1907/1905/ch08.htm.

9. "Quotable Women for Peace," http://www.womeninworldhistory.com/lesson14.html.

10. Aleksei Tarasov-Rodionov, *February 1917* (New York: Covici-Friede, 1931), 46–47, cited in Dale Ross, "The Role of the Women of Petrograd in War, Revolution and Counter-Revolution, 1914-1921" (PhD diss., Rutgers University, 1973), 28.

11. Rosa Luxemburg, *Rosa Luxemburg Speaks* (New York: Pathfinder, 1970), 391.

12. For overviews of the changes leading up to the Women's War, see Robin P. Chapdelaine, "A History of Child Trafficking in Southeastern Nigeria, 1900 to 1930" (PhD diss., Rutgers University, 2014).

13. For a comprehensive account of the issues involved in the Process of colonization and the Women's War, consult Nina Emma Mba, *Nigerian Women Mobilized: Women's Political Activity in Southern Nigeria, 1900-1965* (Berkley: Institute of International Studies, 1982), 68–97; and Marc Matera, Misty L. Bastian, and Susan Kingsley Kent, *The Women's War of 1929: Gender and Violence in Colonial Nigeria* (New York: Palgrave Macmillan, 2012).

14. Derek J. Waller, *The Kiangsi Soviet Republic: Mao and the National Congresses of 1931 and 1934*, Center for Chinese Studies. China Research Monograph 10 (Berkeley: University of California Press, 1973), 28, 30, 31–32.

CHAPTER 6

1. "Gandhi in South Africa," *Encounter South Africa*, http://www.encounter.co.za/article/112.html.

2. *To Honour Women's Day: Profiles of Leading Women in the South African and Namibian Liberation Struggles* (Johannesburg: International Defence and Aid Fund for Southern Africa in cooperation with United Nations Centre Against Apartheid, August 1981), 30.

3. Frances Baard, *My Spirit Is Not Censored: Frances Baard as Told to Barbie Schreiner* (Harare, Zimbabwe: Zimbabwe Publishing House, 1986); reproduced in South African History Online (SAHO) as *My Spirit Is Not Banned*, Part 1, http://www.sahistory.org.za/archive/part-1.

4. Baard, *My Spirit Is Not Banned*, Part 2, "The ANC and the Women's League," http://www.sahistory.org.za/archive/anc-and-womens-league.

5. Ibid., Part 2, "Trade Unions," http://www.sahistory.org.za/archive/trade-unions.

6. Ibid.

7. Joseph Lelyveld, *Great Soul: Mahatma Gandhi and His Struggle with India* (New York: Alfred A. Knopf, 2011), 140.

8. Geneva Convention Relative to the Treatment of Prisoners of War. Adopted on 12 August 1949 by the Diplomatic Conference for the Establishment of International Conventions for the Protection of Victims of War, held in Geneva from April 21 to August 12, 1949, entry into force October 21, 1950, https://www.un.org/en/preventgenocide/rwanda/text-images/Geneva_POW.pdf.

9. Baard, *My Spirit Is Not Banned*, Part 2, "The Program for Action," http://www.sahistory.org.za/archive/anc-and-womens-league.

10. Leo Kuper, *Passive Resistance in South* Africa (London: Jonathan Cape, 1956), 106n7.

11. Ibid.

12. Gary F. Baines, *A History of New Brighton, Port Elizabeth, South Africa 1903-1953: The Detroit of the Union* (Lewiston, NY: Edwin Mellen Press, 2002), 264.

13. *To Honour Women's Day*, 17, 37; Cherryl Walker, *Women and Resistance in South Africa* (New York: Monthly Review Press, 1991), 137.

14. SAHO, "Annie Silinga," http://www.sahistory.org.za/people/annie-silinga.

15. SAHO, "A Documentary History of South African Indians, 72. The Defiance Campaign, 1952," http://www.sahistory.org.za/archive/72-defiance-campaign-1952.

16. SAHO, "A Documentary History of South African Indians, 74. The Freedom Charter, 1955," http://www.sahistory.org.za/archive/74-freedom-charter-1955.

17. Nelson Mandela, *Long Walk to Freedom* (Boston: Little Brown, 1994), 151–52.

18. Walker, *Women and Resistance in South Africa*, 137.

19. *To Honour Women's Day*, 37.

20. Charles Payne, *I've Got the Light of Freedom: The Organizing Tradition and the Mississippi Freedom Struggle* (Berkeley: University of California Press, 1997), 68–72.

21. JoAnn Robinson, *The Montgomery Bus Boycott and the Women Who Started It* (Knoxville: University of Tennessee Press, 1987).

22. David J. Garrow, Introduction to JoAnn Robinson, *The Montgomery Bus Boycott, and the Women Who Started It* (Knoxville: University of Tennessee Press, 1987), ix–x.

23. Townsend Davis, *Weary Feet, Rested Souls: A Guided History of the Civil Rights Movement* (New York: W. W. Norton and Company, 1998).

24. Howell Raines, *My Soul Is Rested: Movement Days in the Deep South Remembered* (Hammondsworth, Middlesex, England: Penguin Books, 1983), 43–44.

25. Raines, *My Soul Is Rested*, 40–42.

26. Robinson, *The Montgomery Bus Boycott*, 44–45; Raines, *My Soul Is Rested*, 46.

27. Raines, *My Soul Is Rested*, 47–48.

28. Robinson, *The Montgomery Bus Boycott*, 39.

29. Pamela E. Brooks, *Boycotts, Buses, and Passes: Black Women's Resistance in the U.S. South and South Africa* (Amherst: University of Massachusetts Press, 2008), 179–201; see also Jacqueline Castledine, "'In a Solid Bond of Unity': Anticolonial Feminism in the Cold War Era," *Journal of Women's History* 20, no. 4 (Winter 2008): 57–81.

CHAPTER 7

1. Brian A. Oard, "Mindful Pleasures: Poetry after Auschwitz: What Adorno Really Said and Where He Said It," http://mindfulpleasures.blogspot.com/2011/03/poetry-after-auschwitz-what-adorno.html.

2. Clare White, "Two Responses to Student Protest: Ronald Reagan and Robert Kennedy," in *Student Protest: The Sixties and After*, ed. Gerard J. DeGroot (London and New York: Longman, 1998), 117–30, at 117.

3. J. Angus Johnston, "Student Activism in the United States before 1960: An Overview," in *Student Protest*, 12–26, at 22–23.

4. Jeremy Rifkin, *The European Dream: How Europe's Vision of the Future Is Quietly Eclipsing the American Dream* (New York: Tarcher/Penguin, 2004), 251.

5. Cajo Brendel, "The Working Class Uprising in East-Germany June 1953: Class Struggle against Bolshevism," *Spartacusbond* (June 1953): 1–25, at 4, https://www.marxists.org/archive/brendel/1953/eastgermany.htm.

6. "Uprising in East Germany 1953: Shedding Light on a Major Cold War Flashpoint: A National Security Archive Electronic Briefing Book," ed. Malcolm Byrne; comp. Gregory F. Domber (June 15, 2001), http://www2.gwu.edu/~nsarchiv/NSAEBB/NSAEBB50/.

7. Brendel, "The Working Class Uprising in East-Germany June 1953," 6.

8. Brown v. Board of Education of Topeka (1954), http://www.infoplease.com/us/supreme-court/cases/ar04.html.

9. Global Nonviolent Action Database: German students campaign for democracy (1966–68), http://nvdatabase.swarthmore.edu/content/german-students-campaign-democracy-1966-68.

10. For a general overview of the German student movement's struggles to maintain German Democracy, see Belinda J. Davis, *Changing the World, Changing Oneself: Political Protest and Collective Identitites in West Germany and the U.S. in the 1960s and 1970s* (New York: Berghan, 2010).

11. Maude Bracke, "French Responses to the Prague Spring: Connections, (Mis)perception and Appriation," *Europe-Asia Studies* 60, no. 10 (December 2008): 1735–47.

12. "Vaclav Havel quotes," http://thinkexist.com/quotes/vaclav_havel/.

13. Gerd-Rainer Horn, "The Working-Class Dimension of 1968," in *Transnational Moments of Change: Europe 1945, 1968, 1989*, ed. Gerd-Rainer Horn and Padraic Kenney (Lanham, MD: Roman & Littlefield Publishers, 2004), 111–12.

14. Dermot Sreenan, "Paris 1968, 25 years ago: When France Rebelled," *Workers Solidarity* No. 39, 1993," http://struggle.ws/ws93/paris39.html.

15. Ibid.

16. Arthur Marwick, " '1968' and the Cultural Revolution of the Long Sixties (c.1958–c.1974)," in *Transnational Moments of Change*, 81–94, at 84.

17. Sreenan, "Paris 1968."

18. Charles Posner, *Reflections on the Revolution in France: 1968* (Harmondsworth, UK: Penguin, 1970), 73; Sreenan, "Paris 1968."

19. Daniel Singer, *Prelude to Revolution: France in May 1968* (New York: Hill and Wang, 1970), 9–10.

20. Posner, *Reflections on the Revolution in France*, 104.

21. Zolov, *Refried Elvis: The Rise of the Mexican Counterculture* (Berkeley: University of California Press, 1999), 119–31.

22. Ibid., 72–77.

23. Ibid., 74–75; Elena Poniatowska, *Massacre in Mexico*, trans. Helen R. Lane (New York: Viking, 1971), 288.

24. Poniatowska, *Massacre in Mexico*, 24–25.

25. Ibid., 45.

26. Ronald L. Ecker, "The Tlatelolco Massacre in Mexico," 6, http://ronecker. byethost18.com/massacre.html.

27. Poniatowska, *Massacre in Mexico*, 88.

28. Ecker, "The Tlatelolco Massacre in Mexico," 7.

29. "Informe Histórico a la Sociedad Mexicana-2006," *Fiscalía Especial para Movimientos Sociales y Políticos del Pasada* (November 2006): 121, 139, cited in Ecker, "The Tlatelolco Massacre in Mexico," 7.

30. Wangari Muta Maathai, *Unbowed: A Memoir* (New York: Anchor Books, 2007), 121.

31. Ibid., 125.

CHAPTER 8

1. Temma Kaplan, *Taking Back the Streets: Women, Youth, and Direct Democracy* (Berkeley: University of California Press, 2003), 195–201.

2. Raj Kumar, Rameshwari Devi, and Romila Pruthi, *Women's Role in [sic] Indian National Movement* (Jaipur, India: Pointer Publishers, 2003), 42–43.

3. Roman Laba, *The Roots of Solidarity: A Political Sociology of Poland's Working-Class Democratization* (Princeton: Princeton University Press, 1991), 21.

4. Ibid., 81.

5. Lawrence Goodwyn, *Breaking the Barrier: The Rise of Solidarity in Poland* (New York: Oxford University Press, 1991), 160.

6. Ibid., 163.

7. Rudolf Diaz, "Socio-Economic Inequality in Chile," *Harvard International Review* (December 22, 2010), http://hir.harvard.edu/pressing-change/socioeconomic-inequality-in-chile-0.

8. Kaplan, *Taking Back the Streets*, 55–56.

9. The entire speech appears in https://www.marxists.org/archive/allende/1973/september/11.htm.

10. Zhang Liang, Andrew Nathan, and Perry Link, eds., *The Tiananmen Papers: The Chinese Leadership's Decision to Use Force against Their Own People—in Their Own Words* (Cambridge, MA: Public Affairs, Perseus Group, 2001), 16.

11. Ibid., 37, 101.

12. Ibid., 114.

13. Kurt Schock, *Unarmed Insurrections: People Power Movements in Nondemocracies: Social Movements, Protest and Contestation* (Minneapolis: University of Minnesota Press, 2005), 99–101.

14. Craig Calhoun, *Neither Gods Nor Emperors: Students and the Struggle for Democracy in China* (Berkeley: University of California Press, 1994), 107–10.

15. Monique Skidmore, "Aung San Suu Kyi," in *Encyclopedia of Human Rights*, ed. David P. Forsythe, 3 Vols. (Oxford, UK: Oxford University Press, 2009), 1:126–29.

16. An important assessment of how the democratic transition proceeded in Burma appears in Evan Osnos, "Letter from Rangoon: The Burmese Spring," *The New Yorker* (August 6, 2012): 52–64.

17. Personal conversation at the New York Institute for the Humanities at New York University, October 1982.

18. A sampling of participant accounts of these movements can be found in Mark Bray, *Translating Anarchy: The Anarchism of Occupy Wall Street* (Winchester, UK: Zero Books, 2013); *Arab Spring Dreams: The Next Generation Speaks Out for Freedom and Justice from North Africa to Iran*, ed. Nasser Weddady and Sohrab Ahmari (New York: Palgrave Macmillan, 2012); and *Diaries of an Unfinished Revolution: Voices from Tunis to Damascus*, ed. Layla Al-Zubaidi, Matthew Cassel, and Nemonie Craven Roderick (New York: Penguin Books, 2013).

Further Reading

CHAPTER 1: PARTING THE WATERS AND ORGANIZING THE PEOPLE

Allam, Schafik. *Everyday Life in Ancient Egypt*. Guizeh, Egypt: Ministry of Culture, Egypt Foreign Cultural Relations, Prism Publications, 1985.

Casson, Lionel. *Everyday Life in Ancient Egypt*. 2nd ed. Baltimore: Johns Hopkins University Press, 2001.

Crone, Patricia. *God's Rule: Government and Islam*. New York: Columbia University Press, 2004.

Finley, M. I. *The Ancient Greeks*. 1963. Reprint, New York: Penguin Books, 1991.

Fornara, Charles W., and Loren J. Samons II. *Athens from Cleisthenes to Pericles*. Berkeley: University of California Press, 1991.

Kagan, Donald. *Pericles of Athens and the Birth of Democracy*. New York: Free Press, 1991.

Kennedy, Hugh. *The Prophet and the Age of the Caliphate: The Islamic Near East from the Sixth to the Eleventh Century*. 2nd ed. New York: Longman, 2004.

Linebaugh, Peter. *The Magna Carta Manifesto: Liberties and Commons for All*. Berkeley: University of California Press, 2008.

Quilter, Jeffrey, and Luis Jaime Castillo Butters, eds. *New Perspectives on Moche Political Organization*. Washington, DC: Dumbarton Oaks Research Library and Collection, 2010.

Woodruff, Paul. *First Democracy: The Challenge of an Ancient Idea*. New York: Oxford University Press, 2005.

CHAPTER 2: PROPHETIC MOVEMENTS AND CITIES OF PROMISE

Espinosa, Aurelio. *The Empire of the Cities: Emperor Charles V, the Communero Revolt, and the Transformation of the Spanish System*. Leiden and Boston: Brill, 2009.

Grewal, J. S. *The Sikhs: Ideology, Institutions, and Identity*. New Delhi: Oxford University Press, 2009.

Haliczer, Stephen. *The Comuneros of Castile: The Forging of a Revolution 1475-1521*. Madison: University of Wisconsin Press, 1981.

Hill, Christopher. *The World Turned Upside Down: Radical Ideas During the English Revolution*. New York: Penguin, 1984.

McLeod, W. H. *Sikhs and Sikhism: The Sikhs: History, Religion, and Society*. New York: Columbia University Press, 1989.

Singh, Khushwant. *A History of the Sikhs*, Vol. I: *1469-1839*. Princeton: Princeton University Press, 1963.

CHAPTER 3: DEMOCRACY AGAINST ALL ODDS

Alden, Dauril. "Late Colonial Brazil, 1750-1808." In *Colonial Brazil*, edited by Leslie Bethell, 284-343. New York: Cambridge University Press, 1987.

Beckstrand, Lisa. *Deviant Women of the French Revolution and the Rise of Feminism*. Madison, NJ: Fairleigh Dickinson University Press, 2009.

Bergad, Laird W. *Slavery and the Demographic and Economic History of Minas Gerais, Brazil, 1720-1888*. Cambridge: Cambridge University Press, 1999.

Fischer, David Hackett. *Paul Revere's Ride*. New York: Oxford University Press, 1994.

Forbes, Esther. *Paul Revere & The World He Lived In*. New York: Houghton Mifflin Harcourt, 1942. Reprint, Boston: Mariner Books, 1999.

Godineau, Dominique. *The Women of Paris and Their French Revolution*. Translated by Katherine Streip. Paris: ALINEA, 1988; Berkeley: University of California Press, 1998.

Levy, Darline Gay, Harriet Branson Applewhite, and Mary Durham Johnson. *Women in Revolutionary Paris, 1789-95*. Urbana: University of Illinois Press, 1979.

Maxwell, Kenneth. *Conflicts and Conspiracies: Brazil and Portugal, 1750-1808*. New York: Routledge, 2004.

Nash, Gary B. *The Forgotten Fifth: African Americans in the Age of Revolution*. Cambridge, MA: Harvard University Press, 2006.

Russel-Wood, A. J. R. *The Black Man in Slavery and Freedom in Colonial Brazil*. New York: St. Martin's, 1982.

Scott, Joan Wallach. *Only Paradoxes to Offer: French Feminists and the Rights of Man*. Cambridge, MA: Harvard University Press, 1996.

CHAPTER 4: WHICH PEOPLE SHALL RULE?

Chase, Malcolm. *Chartism: A New History*. Manchester: Manchester University Press, 2007.

Davin, Delia. *Woman-Work: Women and the Party in Revolutionary China*. Oxford: Clarendon Press, 1976.

Ferrer, Ada. *Insurgent Cuba: Race, Nation and Revolution, 1868-1898*. Chapel Hill: University of North Carolina Press, 1999.

Foner, Philip S. *Antonio Maceo. The "Bronze Titan" of Cuba's Struggle for Independence*. New York: Monthly Review Press, 1977.

Gornick, Vivian. *The Solitude of Self: Thinking about Elizabeth Cady Stanton*. New York: Farrar, Straus and Giroux, 2005.

Hanley, Wayne. *The Genesis of Napoleonic Propaganda, 1796-1799*. New York: Columbia University Press, 2002.

Kazuko, Ono. *Chinese Women in a Century of Revolution, 1850-1950*. Translated and edited by Joshua A. Fogel. Stanford: Stanford University Press, 1988.

Robertson, Priscilla. *Revolutions of 1848: A Social History*. Princeton: Princeton University Press, 1952.

Spence, Jonathan. *God's Chinese Son: The Taiping Heavenly Kingdom of Hong Xiuquan*. New York: Norton, 1996.

Sperber, Jonathan. *European Revolutions 1848-1851*. 2nd ed. New York: Cambridge University Press, 2005.

CHAPTER 5: SOCIAL REVOLUTION AND PARTICIPATORY DEMOCRACY

Addams, Jane, Emily G. Balch, and Alice Hamilton. *Women at the Hague: The International Congress of Women and Its Result*. 1915. Reprint, Urbana: University of Illinois Press, 2003.

Brunk, Samuel. *Emilio Zapata, Revolutionary Betrayal in Mexico.* Albuquerque: University of New Mexico Press, 1995.

Cott, Nancy F. *The Grounding of Modern Feminism.* New Haven: Yale University Press, 1987.

Franke, Wolfgang. *A Century of Chinese Revolution, 1851-1949.* Columbia: University of South Carolina Press, 1980.

Johnson, Kay Ann. *Women and the Family and Peasant Revolution in China.* Chicago: University of Chicago Press, 1983.

Luxemburg, Rosa. *Rosa Luxemburg Speaks.* New York: Pathfinder, 1970.

Macías, Anna. "Women and the Mexican Revolution, 1910-1920." *The Americas* 36, no. 11 (1980): 53–82.

Matera, Marc, Misty L. Bastian, and Susan Kingsley Kent. *The Women's War of 1929: Gender and Violence in Colonial Nigeria.* New York: Palgrave Macmillan, 2012.

Offen, Karen. *Globalizing Feminisms, 1789-1945: Rewriting History.* New York: Routledge, 2010.

Okonjo, Kamene. "The Dual-Sex Political System in Operation: Igbo Women and Community Politics in Midwestern Nigeria." In *Women in Africa:Studies in Social and Economic Change*, edited by Nancy J. Hafkin and Edna G. Bay, 45-58. Stanford: Stanford University Press, 1976.

Womack, John, Jr. *Zapata and the Mexican Revolution.* New York: Vintage, 1968.

CHAPTER 6: CIVIL DISOBEDIENCE AND RACIAL JUSTICE

Baard, Frances. *My Spirit Is Not Censored: Frances Baard as told to Barbie Schreiner.* Harare: Zimbabwe Publishing House, 1986. Reprinted in SAHO: South African History Online: Toward a People's History, http://www.sahistory.org.za/.

Branch, Taylor. *Parting the Waters: America in the King Years: 1953-63.* New York: Simon and Schuster, 1988.

Brooks, Pamela E. *Boycotts, Buses, and Passes: Black Women's Resistance in the U.S. South and South Africa.* Amherst: University of Massachusetts Press, 2008.

Hassim, Shireen. *Women's Organizations and Democracy in South Africa: Contesting Authority.* Madison: University of Wisconsin Press, 2006.

Lelyveld, Joseph. *Great Soul: Mahatma Gandhi and His Struggle with India.* New York: Knopf, 2011.

Mandela, Nelson. *Long Walk to Freedom.* Boston: Little Brown, 1994.

Payne, Charles. *I've Got the Light of Freedom: The Organizing Tradition and the Mississippi Freedom Struggle.* Berkeley: University of California Press, 1997.

Robinson, JoAnn. *The Montgomery Bus Boycott, and the Women Who Started It.* Knoxville: University of Tennessee Press, 1987.

CHAPTER 7: OPTIMISM AND OUTRAGE IN STRUGGLES FOR DEMOCRACY

Davis, Belinda J. *Changing the World, Changing Oneself: Political Protest and Collective Identitites in West Germany and the U.S. in the 1960s and 1970s.* New York: Berghahn, 2010.

DeGroot, Gerard J., ed. *Student Protest: The Sixties and After.* London and New York: Longman, 1998.

Eley, Geoff. *Forging Democracy: The History of the Left in Europe, 1850-2000.* Oxford and New York: Oxford University Press, 2002.

Horn, Gerd-Rainer, and Padraic Kenney, eds. *Transnational Moments of Change: Europe 1945, 1968, 1989.* Lanham, MD: Rowman & Littlefield, 2004.

Kenney, Padraic. *1989: Democratic Revolutions at the Cold War's End: A Brief History with Documents.* Boston: Bedford/St. Martin's, 2010.

Maathai, Wangari Muta. *Unbowed: A Memoir.* New York: Anchor, 2007.

Marwick, Arthur. *The Sixties: Cultural Revolution in Britain, France, Italy and the United States, c. 1958 – c. 1974.* Oxford: Oxford University Press, 1998.

Posner, Charles, ed. *Reflections on the Revolution in France: 1968.* New York: Penguin, 1970.

Singer, Daniel. *Prelude to Revolution: France in May 1968.* New York: Hill and Wang, 1970.

Zolov, Eric. *Refried Elvis: The Rise of the Mexican Counterculture.* Berkeley: University of California Press, 1999.

CHAPTER 8: NEW WORLD DAWNING

Ash, Timothy Garton. *The Polish Revolution: Solidarity.* 3rd ed. New Haven: Yale University Press, 2002.

Dinges, John. *The Condor Years: How Pinochet And His Allies Brought Terrorism To Three Continents.* New York: New Press, 2005.

Goodwyn, Lawrence. *Breaking the Barrier: The Rise of Solidarity in Poland.* New York: Oxford University Press, 1991.

Hershatter, Gail. "State of the Field: Women in China's Long Twentieth Century." *Journal of Asian Studies* 63, no. 4 (Nov. 2004): 991–1065.

Kaplan, Temma. *Taking Back the Streets: Women, Youth, and Direct Democracy.* Berkeley: University of California Press, 2004.

Kumar, Raj, Rameshwari Devi, and Romila Pruthi. *Women's Role in [sic] Indian National Movement.* Jaipur, India: Pointer Publishers, 2003.

Michnik, Adam. "Anti-Authoritarian Revolt: A Conversation with Daniel Cohn-Bendit." In *Letters from Freedom: Post-Cold War Realities and Perspectives,* edited by Irena Grudzińska Gross and translated by Jane Cave, 29-67. Berkeley: University of California Press, 1998.

Moran, Jadwiga E. Pieper. *The Politics of Motherhood: Maternity and Women's Rights in Twentieth-Century Chile.* Pittsburgh: University of Pittsburgh Press, 2009.

Ogden, Suzanne, Kathleen Hartford, Lawrence Sullivan, and David Zweig, eds. *China's Search for Democracy: The Student and the Mass Movement of 1989.* Armonk, NY: M. E. Sharpe, 1992.

Penn, Shana. *Solidarity's Secret: The Women Who Defeated Communism in Poland.* Ann Arbor: University of Michigan Press, 2005.

Radcliff, Pamela Beth. *Making Democratic Citizens in Spain: Civil Society and the Popular Origins of the Transition, 1960-78.* New York: Palgrave Macmillan, 2011.

Skidmore, Monique. *Karaoke Fascism: Burma and the Politics of Fear.* Philadelphia: University of Pennsylvania Press, 2004.

Weddady, Nasser, and Sohrab Ahmari. *Arab Spring Dreams: The Next Generation Speaks out for Freedom and Justice from North Africa to Iran.* New York: Palgrave Macmillan, 2012.

Zhang Liang, Andrew J. Nathan, and Perry Link, eds. *The Tiananmen Papers.* New York: Public Affairs, 2001.

Websites

Avalon Project, Yale University
http://avalon.law.yale.edu/
This site gathers legal, historical, and government documents from 4000 BCE to the present, and includes documentation on ancient Roman efforts to democratize landholding; medieval and early modern charters and constitutions extending democracy to different groups of citizens; letters and articles assessing the movement toward independence in the American colonies and formation of the Constitution; treaties and official documents concerned with slavery; the Hague Peace Conference of 1894 and related letters and reports; papers dealing with efforts to establish new states in the Middle East between 1916 and 2001; and a collection of documents from the Nuremberg Trials at the end of the Second World War.

Discovering American Women's History Online
http://digital.mtsu.edu/cdm/landingpage/collection/women
In documents ranging from the activities of craftswomen, to women's representation in advertising, to their oral testimonies about lives under slavery, or as Japanese Americans before, during, and after the Second World War, this unique collection of primary documents is maintained by Ken Middleton, the librarian at Middle Tennessee State University's Walter Library.

Historical Newspapers Online
http://libguides.bgsu.edu/content.php?pid=478027
This multilingual site, from Bowling Green State University (BGSU), includes ICON (International Coalition on Newspapers) the Newspaper Digitation Project of newspapers worldwide that features material on political changes; Wartime Press World War Two archives, including views about the War's democratic goals; and History Buff Newspaper Archives about important political events from 1707 to 1994, arranged chronologically.

The History Workshop, Vanderbilt University
http://researchguides.library.vanderbilt.edu/content.php?pid=527161&sid=4633019
This primary source database provides material on Slavery and Social Justice from 1490 to 2007 and the Early American Digital Archive (EADA) of the Maryland Institute for Technology in the Humanities.

Internet History Sourcebooks Project
www.fordham.edu/Halsall/
This resource includes a wide range of primary documents, including travelers' reports, from the ancient to the modern period in Africa, East Asia, the Middle East, Europe, Latin America, and North America.

National Security Archive
www2.gwu.edu/~nsarchiv/
Housed at George Washington University in Washington, DC, this collection consists of declassified US government documents ranging from consideration of the Cuban Missile Crisis to the Rwanda genocide, secured through the Freedom of Information Act.

Perseus Digital Library
www.perseus.tufts.edu/
This site holds a growing collection of online resources for studying the ancient world. Materials include ancient texts and translations, maps, articles, essays, and images from more than seventy museums around the world.

Primary Documents On-line (CSUSM)
https://library.csusm.edu/subject_guides/history/online_primary.asp
The California State University at San Marcos' website includes important primary sources and oral histories from Europe, Latin America, Africa, the Middle East, East Asia, South Asia, the Pacific Rim, and the United States including Sources and General Resources on Latin America and Proceedings of the Old Bailey 1674–1837, which provides testimonies from Britain's main criminal court demonstrating how democracy worked and did not work among the English poor.

SAHO: South African History Online: Toward a People's History
www.sahistory.org.za/
This site contains extensive primary sources about South Africa from its early history through its first democratic election in 1994. It includes newspaper accounts, legal documents, and over four thousand biographies of activists who pursued the struggle for democracy. Special sections deal with the documentary history of the Indian community in South Africa.

Vietnam Center and Archive
www.vietnam.ttu.edu
Housed at Texas Tech University, this site includes numerous pages of written documents and photographs, slides, maps, periodicals, films, recordings, and books related to the Vietnam War, Indochina, and the war's impact on the United States and Southeast Asia.

World History Matters
http://worldhistorymatters.org/
The Roy Rosenzweig Center for History and New Media at George Mason University has developed a website with a series of primary sources, including images, jokes, first-hand accounts, and memoirs about the French Revolution, the eruption of movements for democracy in 1989 in Eastern Europe, accounts of life in the Gulags or prison camps of the Soviet Union, and women's movements worldwide. Supplementing the primary sources are discussions of class presentations and teaching modules.

Women's Social Movements, International—1840 to the Present
http://wasi.alexanderstreet.com/
Focusing on women's activism in unions, peace movements, and other forms of collective action, the website includes conference proceedings, letters, journals, and scholarly articles that analyze the activities of women's formation of international associations.

Acknowledgments

Thanks to Ellen Broidy, David Carpenter, Paula Covington, Dick Glendon, Vishal Kamath, Sara Kozameh, Steven McGrail, Lynn Mally, Robert G. Moeller, Margaret Power, Ellen Ross, Margaret Strobel, and Barbara Weinstein for seeing this through, and special thanks to Rebecca Hecht, Nancy Toff, Kate Nunn, and Andrew Joseph Westerhaus for getting it into print.

Chronological Volumes

The World from Beginnings to 4000 BCE
The World from 4000 to 1000 BCE
The World from 1000 BCE to 500 CE
The World from 300 to 1000 CE
The World from 1000 to1500
The World from 1450 to1700
The World in the Eighteenth Century
The World in the Nineteenth Century
The World in the Twentieth Century

Thematic and Topical Volumes

The City: A World History
Democracy: A World History
Food: A World History
Empires: A World History
The Family: A World History
Genocide: A World History
Health and Medicine: A World History
Migration: A World History
Race: A World History
Technology: A World History

Geographical Volumes

The Atlantic in World History
Central Asia in World History
China in World History
The Indian Ocean in World History
Japan in World History
Mexico in World History
Russia in World History
The Silk Road in World History
South Africa in World History
South Asia in World History
Southeast Asia in World History
Trans-Saharan Africa in World History

Index

direct democracy, 2–3
divorce, 112–13
Douglass, Frederick, 54–55
Dubček, Alexander, 100
Dutschke, Rudi, 99, 103
Dylan, Bob, 99

Edes, Benjamin, 32
Edes, Joseph, 32
education, 95–96, 98–99, 102. *See also*
    student demonstrations
Egypt, 7, 113, 125–26
England: American Revolution and,
    33–36; Levellers and, 26–30; Nigeria
    and, 72–74; Norman Conquest of, 17;
    South Africa and, 78, 80–81
Ephigenia of the Cross, St., 44

Falcón, Lydia, 112
Federal Republic of Germany (BRD, West
    Germany), 96, 99–100, 102
Ferdinand, Emperor of Austria, 52
Ferdinand II, King of Aragon, 21–22
feudalism, 49
Finland, 58
France: education in, 102; French
    Revolution and, 36–39, 44–45;
    migrations to, 96; suffragist movements
    in, 66; Vietnam and, 101–2
Franco, Francisco, 112
Frederick Barbarossa, Holy Roman
    Emperor, 51
freedom of speech and publication, 3
French Revolution, 36–39, 44–45
fueros (charters), 16

Gaddafi, Muammar, 125
Galindo, Hermila, 66
Gandhi, Manilal, 79
Gandhi, Mohandas Karamchand
    (Mahatma): in India, 83–84, *84*, 113; in
    South Africa, 77, 79, 90
Garrison, William Lloyd, 37
Garzón, Balthazar, 120
Gaulle, Charles de, 102, 105
genital cutting, 113
German Democratic Republic (GDR, East
    Germany), 96, 97–98
Germanic peoples, 13–14
Germany, 52, 85–86, 100. *See also*
    Federal Republic of Germany (BRD,
    West Germany); German Democratic
    Republic (GDR, East Germany)
Gill, John, 32
Goebbels, Josef, 85
Goering, Hermann, 85
Gómez, Máximo, 58
Gorbachev, Mikhail, 116
Gouges, Olympe de, 37

Gracchus, Gaius, 11, *12*, 13
Gracchus, Tiberius, 11–13, *12*
grass-roots organizations, 32
Great Leap Forward (China), 121
Greece, 7–11, 126
Guadeloupe, 53

Haiti, 37
Hakka people, 56
Hammurabi of Babylonia, 5–6, *6*
Havel, Václav, 100
Henry II, King of England, 17
Henry VIII, King of England, 26–27
Hidalgo, Miguel, 47, *48*
higher education, 95–96
Hindu caste system, 20
Hinduism, 19–21
Hirohito, Japanese Emperor, 85
Hitler, Adolph, 85, 100
Ho Chi Minh, 101
Holland, 96
Honduras, 61
Hong Jen-kan (Hong Rengan), 57–58
Hong Xiuquan, 56
Horton, Myles, 91
Hu Yaobang, 121
human rights, 86
hunger strikes, 110, 122
Hutchinson, Thomas, 34

imam (spiritual leader), 15–16
India, 77, 83–85, 96, 113
indigenous people, 36
Indochinese Communist Party, 101
International Military Tribunal at
    Nuremberg, 85–86
internet, 3
Iran, 99
Iraq, 15. *See also* Mesopotamia
Isabella I, Queen of Castile, 21–22
Islam, 14, 15–16, 20–21
Italy, 50, 51–52, 85. *See also* Roman
    Empire; Roman Republic

Jacobs, Aletta, 70
Japan, 83, 85
Jaruzelski, Wojciech, 116
Jefferson, Thomas, 43
Jesus of Nazareth, 14
Jews, 21–22
Jiménez y Muro, Dolores, *65*
Jodl, Alfred, 85
John, King of England, 17
John Paul II, Pope, 115
Joseph, St. (São José), 44
Juana, Queen of Castile and León, 22
Juárez, Benito, 49
Judaism, 14
juntas (governing committees), 47

9 780195 338089